THE
CHARACTERS
OF
CREATIVITY

ALASTAIR PEARCE

BIS PUBLISHERS

BIS Publishers
Borneostraat 80-A
1094 CP Amsterdam
The Netherlands
T +31 (0)20 515 02 30
bis@bispublishers.com
www.bispublishers.com

ISBN 9789063696696
Copyright © 2023 Alastair Pearce and BIS Publishers

CONTENTS

INTRODUCTION

This book is a practical guide for managers and colleagues of creative people. It is my attempt at deepening the quality of creativity at work whilst diminishing the amount stifled at birth by poor management or insensitive colleagues.

The analysis and subsequent advice offered here is based on my own long experience of working with creative people, first as a colleague, then as their manager and latterly as head of the organisation. The research that underpins this book is therefore qualitative rather than quantitative, and, just like the creative process itself, indeterminate, chaotic, divergent, non-instrumental and all just a bit random. My audacity in suggesting that I might be able to help you in working with your creatives relies simply on the fact that if I learnt how to do it, you can too. And, with my help, I trust you will accumulate the necessary skills rather more quickly than I did.

The practical nature of my aim and my 'research' means that the starting point for discussing creativity is not the brain's chemical peculiarities that those people labelled 'creative' are said to possess, nor is it the psychological origins of the many and various distinctive characteristics that creatives frequently display through their work. No, my observations kick off where those investigations into the origins of creativity end. They started for me at the same point at which they probably start for you: the moment you meet a new colleague at work who turns out to be rather creative. Perhaps he or she was explicitly employed to be creative; perhaps not.

'He or she'. I'll get this out of the way right now. In my view there is no relationship between gender and creativity, nor is there between any particular style or focus of creativity and the gender of the creative person. However, in this book you will see I do allocate a gender to creative caricatures. The allocation is random and undertaken simply to avoid the tedious 'he or she', and the only mildly better 'he/she'. Additionally, my justification for assigning genders as well as names to the caricatures – Playful, Molotov, Solo, Artiste, Monk, and all the rest who are woven through the book in chapters of their own – is a desire on my part to breathe some humanity into these bloodless ciphers in the hope that you will recognise their characteristics having seen them displayed every day at work by colleagues who do indeed have names and probably genders.

The structure of this book alternates between sketches of creative traits – the named and gendered caricatures – and more conventional discussions of creativity. All end with advice on how the colleague or manager keen to promote creativity might act. The more conventional chapters inevitably rely heavily on the work of other scholars. A short list of sources cited is provided, but it is only fair to identify Gordon Torr's magnificent and very readable book, *Managing Creative People*, as the origin and prompter of many ideas here examined. The chapters that introduce the creative caricatures are however my own dangerous innovation. I'll tell you how I came to invent them before explaining how to avoid their dangers.

My career started in earnest as a lecturer in music at a university in the middle of England (I'm glazing over my stint as a deliverer of newspapers and a disastrous spell misunderstanding computers at Oxford University). As an academic musician working within a faculty principally concerned with the practical making of music, I was among creative colleagues whose ways of working seemed all just a bit chaotic to me – albeit a delightful change from the algorithms of Oxford. I set about trying to insert some of my conventional order into this disorder. I now regret this, for I was attempting to dismantle a key characteristic of creativity: apparent chaos. Anyway, universities are big organisations run by serious people with conventional ideas of 'good' management, so I was rapidly promoted to increasingly senior levels in the music school. But I wasn't totally blind to what my colleagues were actually trying to do and the ways they were doing it. They were hard working, obsessed – sorry, that's my conventional interpretation – no, they were dedicated to guarding the long-evolved pedagogy and practice of their art from intruders, like me. Their other characteristics often included: fears about their own ongoing abilities as creatives; a sense of playfulness; a protective attitude to the products of their creativity; a mistrust of evaluation and other manifestations of 'management'; a blind eye for deadlines; and a common preference for working alone reflected in an awkwardness in teams beyond the perceived boundaries of their discipline. Course validation events were therefore not popular; rehearsing string quartets, fine.

I was then asked by the head of my university to negotiate the entry of a local private drama college into our organisation. My musical colleagues warned against the plan: "They're so different from us!" You've guessed what I found: fears about ongoing creativity; playfulness; protectiveness; mistrust of 'management'; the same blindspot for deadlines; and a common preference for creating alone. I was learning…

Next, as principal of a drama college in London, no longer working with musicians but amidst the same preoccupations. Then, as president of Singapore's major international arts college. Lots of different disciplines, all unique in their practice but linked by the same characteristics of creative people. You can see now how the births in this book came about: Solo (works best alone); Molotov (fights against management); Wobbly (insecure); Playful (fun but a bit annoying); Artiste (hyper-protective of the objects she creates); and all the rest. They are the common characteristics of the creatives I have been privileged to work with time and time again but now distilled into fictional distinct caricatures of creativity.

This distillation has the advantage of being able to focus on a single characteristic leading to specific comments on how colleagues and managers might best react. The name with which I have awarded each caricature is, of course, suggestive of the creative characteristic being examined. But it's a dangerous method, and I suspect its advantages only just outweigh its negative elements. I've noticed that friends testing the caricatures often say things like: "Oh yeah, I'm definitely a Solo...", or "Bill's certainly a Wobbly." Fun, but contorting real life, for all my caricatures are single aspects abstracted from multifaceted human beings. I stress therefore, despite my friends' assertions, that Picky, Wobbly, Molotov *et al* do not exist, and although they have names and genders, have never existed. But they might, I hope, remind you of certain behaviours that your own creative colleagues display from time to time. And, because you understand Picky, Solo or Monk, you will be able to assist your colleagues to deepen their own creativity yet further.

One more danger of my approach: don't mistake the arrow for a boomerang. Whilst many creative people are worried about their own inventiveness, are often playful and chaotic in the ways they work, and are frequently sceptical of management, the reverse is not necessarily true. Many of your colleagues may possess unremarkable powers of creativity but still hate the boss. Having a deep mistrust of management does not therefore mean you're highly creative.

It's important that I acknowledge a tension between creativity itself and my analysis of creativity. This book, in line with the thinking of other writers, observes the process that humans go through to produce an output that might be regarded by others, as well as perhaps themselves, as 'creative'. This process varies massively from one creative person to the next and seems steeped in uncertain psychological and physical influences and unpredictable external and internal factors.

The process may be quick or slow, painful or pleasurable, the solution to a known problem, or an irrelevant stab at a totally disconnected subject. Not surprisingly, for such an indeterminate and uncertain process, creativity seems to thrive best in divergent, even chaotic, environments and to wither when constrained by rules, customs and tradition. Organisations are organised; creativity isn't. How can they possibly work together? And yet, here is a book that champions chaos in organisations and claims it can work! An organisation is structured, measured and usually has agency to define and pursue goals; the creative colleagues it employs are using largely unstructured methods and unmeasurable processes with uncertain agency, apparently in pursuit of those organisational goals. I am not, by the rigour of my 'solutions' attempting to dismantle the inherent spontaneity of creativity or undermine the necessary structure of the organisation. I'm simply trying to get the two working more easily together for the benefit of both. And the conduit for the balm that I'm trying to massage into this interface is the people: the creatives, their colleagues and their managers.

So, that's the first tension that worries its way through this book. A second, linked concern is that I might be attempting to mechanise creativity. No, I'm simply suggesting how organisations can work effectively and happily with their creative colleagues. I set about this by teasing apart certain characteristics of creative people while making no attempt to control, systematise or teach the process of creativity. The book's goal is the release of more and better creativity, and thus a deepening of our respect for creativity as a hugely valuable and mysterious attribute of humanity. An attempt to mechanise creativity would not only undermine the essential humanity and spontaneity of the process, but also, I hope, be doomed to failure.

In a book about creatives, it's obviously more than a little useful to identify who it is we're actually discussing. Chapter 2 *Are we all creative?* goes into the details, but it's worth pointing out here that creatives are not identifiable by the job they do but by how they do the job. So, this book is not simply focused on 'creative' people working in the arts or, more broadly, within 'creative professions' (architects, designers…), but instead casts its gaze still wider to invite all people who bring a sniff of creativity to the way they work.

And the reason I've written this book? I'm a creativity fan. I know that creativity provides solutions to problems and delight to the soul, optimism for the future and fun for today. Who wouldn't be a fan of creativity? Well, apparently lots of people and companies judging by the way creativity is stifled by organisational protocols, well-meaning yet misguided management and colleagues' insensitivity. It is a goal of this book to broaden and deepen humanity's pool of creativity by contesting its suppression and neglect through enriching management and interpersonal practice to the benefit of all.

One final, bathetic apology: 'creative' as a noun rather than just an adjective. I don't like it, I railed against it, but well, language has its own creative and innovative process too, I suppose.

PICKY
"HANG ON A SECOND, THERE'S JUST ONE MORE THING..."

You'll find Picky in many organisations. She's great, works hard and is determined to produce the finest quality creative product she possibly can. She'll say, whilst rushing lunch at her desk: "Well, yes, I suppose I am a bit of a perfectionist." And that's her reputation in the organisation: nothing duff gets past our Picky. Excellent, Pickys are vital for quality. Okay, sometimes she can be a bit annoying when a deadline is approaching, for there's always, always just one more thing that Picky must put right, although the rest of your team knows it's good enough already. But, most of the time you can put up with that.

Picky picks not only at the end of a project but all the way through from conception to delivery, and it's this observation that makes you wonder if 'perfectionist' is really quite the right role-label to pin on her psychological lapel. It's not wrong exactly but not quite the whole story. For Picky is engrossed in the process of creativity more than the product of creativity. To her, the engineering, craft and intellectual challenge of creativity is profoundly satisfying and Picky doesn't want it to stop. Picking at problems – real or invented – is her way of prolonging the fun. So, her title 'perfectionist' isn't wrong exactly – because near-perfection is often the result of her work – but it's a kind of mask she wears over her true identity: Picky.

So, she insists that all contradictory opinions be exhaustively debated, and you notice the way she loves to analyse and critique others' work, to pick at existing problems she's found and predict new ones that haven't yet emerged, if they ever will. For Picky it's crosswords, sudoko and chess rolled into one. The tangible product – just as in those three games – isn't really the point at all, it's the process she enjoys so much.

You notice that Picky – unlike some of the other creatives you work with – isn't really a loner. She's quite happy working in teams, even prefers it, for that interaction with others provides a forum for endless debates with other Pickys; although perhaps you notice that she always insists on getting the last pick. There is one team member, however, with whom she probably dislikes working: Playful. She will probably disapprove of his light-hearted attitude to work, so different from her serious-minded scrutiny of problems. Ironic really, for Playful and Picky are in fact closely related; both are concerned to prolong the fun of their personal creativity, just with very different styles. Picky, under the cover of: "I just have to get this right!" Playful: "What's wrong with a bit of fun?"

Picky is a useful colleague: not only can she be scrupulously creative in her own work, but she is helpful in ensuring team-based projects produce carefully considered results. This rough sketch of her has however revealed that she might at times be tricky to manage: deadlines might slip whilst Picky has 'just one final look'; other colleagues may become irritated at her forensic scrutiny of their work; and budgets might stretch as additional consideration is insisted upon. How might these negative aspects of Picky's work be mitigated? Well, it would surely be unwise to staff a project team solely with Pickys. You can just imagine the endless debates as your Gantt chart withers next to the exhausted water cooler.

A less extreme example of possible mitigation might see a new product being devised that is simply a modification of a successful, tried and tested existing product. Would it, in this situation, be sensible to include Picky in the team? And, even if your answer to that is: "Yes, she'll make sure it works...", when in the development process should her expertise be introduced? I suggest at a comparatively late 'snagging' stage. Although Picky will probably baulk at this, claiming that if she's involved throughout the project there won't be any 'snags' at the end, you may decide that this setback for Picky is a price worth paying for a reliable deadline and the ongoing composure of Picky's colleagues, free – for most of the time – from her superfluous picking.

Sometimes, particularly when working in a team – wisely containing a high proportion of non-Pickys – her colleagues may need to protect themselves from her Picky influence. This might simply prompt their assertion that they're happy with the current state of work. And no, it's not going to be looked at again. On more serious occasions managerial input might be required, such as insisting on a deadline or even the removal of Picky from the team, having thanked her for her creative work, noting that the project is now beyond that stage, and reassuring her that other, younger projects now need her investigative skills.

Although Picky's colleagues are usually the first to complain, this isn't always the case. Sometimes Pickys are able, through their dedication and hard work, to gather a fan club around them who buy into their supererogatory and pedantic picking. I once had a senior colleague in an organisation I attempted to lead, who had set up a mechanism for data checking, storage and inquiry that would have shamed Interpol in its rigour, sophistication and expense. However, I quickly discovered, when pointing out to my Picky that its cost to the organisation massively outweighed its value, that she had successfully convinced her colleagues actually administering the system that this was the most rigorous system imaginable (and it was) and so must be preserved (not so). None of the administrators' jobs were at risk, but I was nevertheless swamped by colleagues all accusing me of having no interest in 'real quality'. I persisted, prevailed, and the world didn't end.

Would Picky be an effective manager of other creative people? Many interview panels would say so, for she is clearly dedicated to quality, keen to be involved in all current projects and enthusiastic about additional avenues of future work. She therefore has a great attitude to work (one that you'd like to see rub off on other colleagues), is in tune with the direction of the company and eager to assist its rollout. 'Perfectionist' into 'perfect manager'? Well, maybe; but only if Picky can develop considerable insight into her own creative motivation and, as a consequence, moderate some of her pickiness when managing others with different motivations. I know a CEO of a large company who indicates on multi-page documents exactly where, and at what angle, he wants his PA to insert the staple on the paper copy. I bet he's fun to work for!

Picky, as a manager of creatives, may well find it hard to recognise that her personal way of being creative is not necessarily the preferred pattern of the creatives for whom she is now responsible. Her use of picking succeeds in structuring her own creative process, allowing her to luxuriate at length within the excitement of it all, but it is unlikely that she consciously understands this. Recall how she proudly, but naively described herself: "Well, yes, I suppose I am a bit of a perfectionist." Picky will therefore find it neither easy nor comfortable externalising that understanding to the extent required to appreciate, and accommodate in her team, alternative processes to creativity.

The result, if she is indeed promoted to become a manager of other creatives but without an enriched perspective on her own practice, may well be micro-management followed by burnout, and frustrated colleagues cornered into processes at odds with their own creative methods. Picky Manager, as opposed to other promoted creatives, is unfortunately susceptible to this clash of psychologies; for Picky's psyche is decidedly unusual in its fascination with detail. Most creatives tend to produce their best work when goals are loosely set (if at all), timescales are flexible, budgets hardly mentioned, and when the gestation of creativity is more a chaotic exploration of a maze than Picky's analytic scrutiny of observable facts. Picky as the manager of such a group of colleagues is a scary prospect.

An interview panel considering her promotion to manager needs to have an unusually self-perceptive Picky, a clear development plan for her, and, in case things go wrong, unusually effective ear defenders against the likely screams of her subordinate colleagues. Safer to leave Picky picking her proven way to her own valuable creativity.

Is Picky's creativity entwined with her pickiness or is she creative despite her pickiness? This might sound like an avoidably theoretical question, but it points towards another, which her manager should certainly ask: "Should I try and get her to be less picky, or will this make her less creative; so is it worth the effort?"

Imagine you are her manager, giving her a new project to work on. Which of these three briefs is the most likely to get the best creative ideas from Picky?

'Please come up with a design for a new soft toy – just the outer covering, we must use the same inside. So, something like an otter using our old snake stuffing.'

'Can you please come up with a toy attractive to children just starting to use social media?'

'Please create the design for a new animated soft toy related to Monkey Business – the new must-watch YouTube channel for 10-year-old children. It must have a rechargeable battery, interactive capability, be impressive on social media, have child-friendly colours and retail for under £20.'

I strongly suspect that the second brief will spark Picky's interest most. This is because it's the most open-ended, giving her the greatest opportunity for picking around the myriad possibilities within the social media market. She will survey and minutely criticise the range of toys already available, find out what children are saying about them on social media, what currently attracts them, and examine the characteristics that could be translated to a physical format. She will doubtless spend more detailed, productive and intrinsically satisfying time in this process than she would exploring the comparatively closed opportunities of the first and last briefs.

Creativity scholars' noses will have twitched at three key words I've recently used: 'maze', 'time' and 'intrinsically'. They will have correctly sniffed that I'm hinting that 'time' spent in what we call 'the maze' with its 'intrinsic' motivation lies at the root of this brief's power in energising Picky's deeper creativity. These complicated ideas of the maze and motivation are discussed in detail in Chapter 8 *Why do I do what I do?* It is sufficient here simply to conclude that Picky's creativity is almost certainly inextricably entwined with her pickiness and her manager would consequently be unwise to try to separate them. If Picky stops picking, she'll probably also stop being creative.

ARE WE ALL CREATIVE?

You are sitting in a restaurant and your table wobbles. You stick a napkin under one of its legs. It stops wobbling. Have you just been creative?

But sitting in restaurants isn't your full-time job. You're a highly respected artist, so after lunch you walk thoughtfully back to your studio wondering about how to solve a particularly difficult problem with your latest portrait; somehow the hands just don't look right. And then, you've got it! Let the hands rest on a book and then that pesky angle between hand and arm comes just right. Have you just been creative?

How do you recognise creativity? Many would say that coming up with the wobbly table solution wasn't creative whilst your walk back to the studio was. That seems to make sense: sticking a napkin under the leg is hardly original; a bit more imaginative than the traditional beer mat, but still pretty obvious. No invention was required, not much effort, thought, or inspiration. None of the characteristics we like to associate with 'proper' creativity: the lonely inventor, striding, tortured, around the laboratory, or the writer huddled over a manuscript pouring out their soul. These are old images but they're still shaping the way we think about creativity today. So, let's strip away that romantic stuff and look at what actually happened in the restaurant and then walking to your studio.

You perceived two problems: wobbly table and duff painted hand. You came up with two solutions: the napkin under the table leg and change the angle of the hand by inserting a book into the painting. Exactly the same process: you perceived a problem and you came up with a solution. So, if the painting's solution was based on creativity, how can we claim the wobbly table wasn't? An obvious difference is 'originality'. Everybody knows how to cure wobbly tables, and all you had to do was apply that knowledge to this particular table using suitable material immediately available: the napkin. But what about your painting? This is different, for it's not commonly known how to sort out a troublesome hand in a portrait.

So is that it? Is it invention – originality – that makes all the difference, one creative, the other one not? Seems likely, but hang on… You are a professional artist. Your training was principally in the craft of painting: not the inventive and arguably unteachable ethereal stuff of imagination, but in the nuts and bolts of how to put paint on canvas and get the wretched stuff to represent what's in your mind. Your craft skills gave you the ability to solve the problem of the misshapen hand. So, your solution to the wobbly table was based on pre-existing knowledge, as was your duff hand solution. Neither were 'inventive' in the way we like to imagine creatives working: that nineteenth century idea of inspiration suddenly striking from a clear blue sky. Creativity and its less glamorous cousin, problem-solving, are not that far apart.

Both your wobbly table solution and the corrected hand were creative. But I'm certainly not saying they were the same. For beyond and above the shared problem-solving component, there probably lies a higher-level creative drive in you the artist, than in you the table fixer, and this psychological need to create can have considerable implications for your personality and what people think about you.

I am able to jog a couple of kilometres if I have to, but put me up against a professional athlete and you can imagine the result. Creativity, like the ability to run, is a spectrum. Your wobbly table answer was at the mundane easy end of the creativity spectrum, whilst your problem-hand solution was much further along. I believe (along with some, but not all academic researchers in creativity) that creativity is an attribute shared by all human beings. Arguably it's one of the key components of our species' rise to dominance (for both good and ill) on our planet.

And this seems a comfortable, egalitarian, liberal, anti-elitist, democratic conclusion. Hey it's great, we're all creatives, wonderful. Not quite that simple I'm afraid. I didn't say we are all the same. I just said we are all on the same spectrum. Sorting out tables and paintings is not the same, just as my geriatric jogging and Olympic medals are at somewhat different ability points.

A spectrum is a scale with two extremes and it is this fact that allows some of those apparently archaic notions listed earlier about creatives still usefully to resonate today. Those who are significantly creative will often present particular personality traits on which their creativity depends. So, some will be allergic to working in teams; some will have a monk-like devotion to their calling and appear infuriatingly inflexible; others will be so wedded to the products of their creativity that they will, at work, appear narcissistic in that they are unreasonably resistant to any criticism, however well intentioned. These are just three traits personified by the caricatures of this book. Perhaps recognisable in colleagues of yours? Tricky to work with, but with the degree of creativity that can not only solve problems but also gestate innovations? These are the colleagues that many companies rely on for new ideas, but who will probably work within organisational structures not designed for loners, inflexibles or those phobic to criticism. Elsewhere in this book I will continue to refer to these people as 'significantly creative' to distinguish them – I confess impressionistically – from those in the more modest regions of the creativity spectrum.

Creativity is, in my view, a function of human intelligence and therefore a potential possessed by all of us. Sure, there is a spectrum of creative abilities just as there is in our ability to play football, do hard sums, or play a musical instrument, but we're all on the spectrum somewhere.

So, I'm not really very worried about the 'we're all creative' *v.* 'creativity is a rare attribute' debate. If we are concerned to promote creativity, there is, within the reality of day to day work, little separating the ways we should interact with our significantly creative colleagues from those used with colleagues not showing many signs of creativity. What I'm saying is the environment for ensuring the flowering of significant creativity and nurturing the first shoots of hidden creativity are generally much the same. So, whether you see creatives as a separate elite species of uniquely gifted humans being distinct from the rest of us problem-solvers, or whether you see a spectrum linking the two groups, it really makes little difference to how we should work with them.

Surely there's an easy way of identifying creatives? Just ask the candidate what organisation he or she works for. If it's a 'creative industry', they're creative; if not, not. Obviously unreliable. Indeed, the crowning of certain industries as 'creative' whilst leaving others tacitly but loudly 'uncreative', has, in my opinion, done more to stifle creativity than any other wound inflicted by the English language.

I once interviewed the manager of a major orchestra. I was seeking his views on how his players could develop their creativity. "Alastair!" he interrupted, "…the last thing we want is for our violinists to be creative; they've all got to do exactly the same thing!" There is a lot of apparently creative activity going on in 'creative industries' that demands distinctly less creativity, often little more than the competent exercise of craft skills. And craft skills tend to be conservative in nature, reinforcing a profession's cohesion; perhaps rather like the violin section of an orchestra. 'Conservative' and 'cohesion' are not words that describe significant creativity.

A barrister defending her client finds a combination of obscure precedents that obliges the judge to direct the jury to a not-guilty verdict. The legal profession is not a 'creative industry'; but that barrister was using significant creativity.

It's clearly a pity that the word 'creativity' is used so promiscuously within some industries, but perhaps its presence above their front doors does at least encourage their lesser creative residents to aspire to greater creativity. So, although it's sad that the word has been loosely applied, it's not actually damaging to creativity. What is dangerous is the reverse: the lack of the word 'creative' in the mindset of a company that is not in a 'creative industry'. Here, the absence of the title can quietly persuade colleagues that their creativity really doesn't matter: "It's not really part of my world…" says the engineer struggling with a sub-optimal mechanical process, "…it's not my job to come up with a better way of doing it." This can spread weedkiller on any tender shoots of creativity that may be struggling towards the light.

SUMMARY

- All humans are creative. A spectrum of creativity stretches from mundane to extraordinary.

- Creativity very often involves problem-solving and this is common across the spectrum.

- The more intense regions of the spectrum are distinguished by a psychologically induced need, a drive, for the individual to create; a psychology that is the basis of the creativity and without which the creativity may be compromised.

- This drive to significant creativity often results in various perceivable character traits that can make working in corporate environments uncomfortable, both for the creative and his or her colleagues.

- Creativity is not the exclusive property of the 'creative industries'; nor is that title a guarantee of its contents.

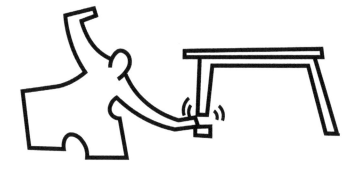

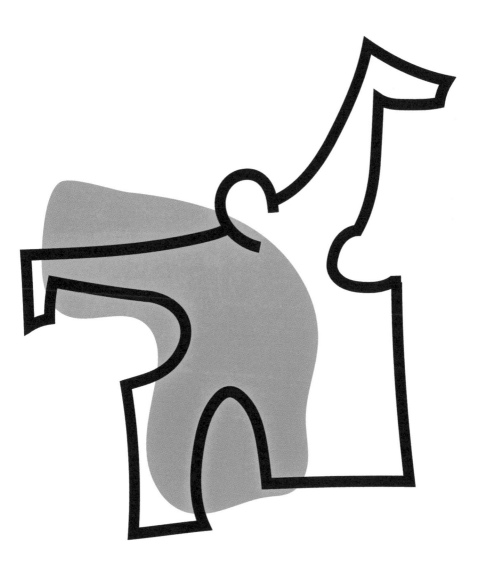

MOLOTOV

"I'M JUST NOT PUTTING UP WITH THIS ANY MORE!"

Molotov detonates hand grenades. She's the creative who demands change in your company and works for it with explosive force.

What is her nickname? Is it Molotov 'the Revolutionary' or how about Molotov 'the Disruptor', or perhaps Molotov 'the Change Agent'? And who gets to choose? Well, no-one decides their own nickname, and this is important; for the soubriquets you and your colleagues choose for Molotov reflect, then frame, your various professional relationships with her. If you see her actions as revolutionary then you'll likely pull up the drawbridge for defensive action; if instead you interpret them as prompts for positive change, then she's a helpful colleague with valuable creative ideas. And if it's Molotov 'the Disruptor' she's bang on trend; for today we all claim – some more plausibly than others – to welcome disruptive ideas. So, Molotov's name and role in your company are defined not by Molotov but by her colleagues, whilst her own, unchangeable, identity comes from her innate need to affect change: the impulse to all creativity.

How can your company cope with Molotov? Well, the flexible nature of her reputation – simultaneously Threat, Asset and Seer – should nudge a management response equally flexible. The company's programme of staff training should encourage colleagues to perceive and react appropriately to the range of Molotov's various roles. This will be particularly useful for Molotov's manager, who will have to adjust his or her own perception of Molotov as her personal objectives seem to shift with different tasks she is given. The manager should also recognise, and probably at times scaffold, Molotov's peers' perceptions of their challenging colleague. Three headings might be useful in such a training programme: recognising Molotov; suitable and unsuitable projects for her; and Molotov in a team.

Recognising Molotov is usually not hard. She's the colleague whose creative ideas seem to be designed to be damaging. Unhelpful disruption appears not so much an unfortunate consequence of her powerful ideas, but rather the goal that the ideas serve. The training here might focus on ways she and her manager might uncouple her idea from its disruptive consequence. When put into practice, a committed Molotov will be annoyed at this exercise, whilst a creative colleague who has simply learned through experience that a belligerent approach can sometimes work, will be surprised and rather relieved.

Assigning suitable projects to Molotov is also quite easy. Her managers simply have to recognise the futility, and probable pain, of putting her on projects that merely develop an existing product. Instead, allowing her to invest her revolutionary drive in new areas that require challenge to the status quo is much wiser. A second area of work in which Molotov could be useful is scanning beyond the company's horizons for signs of competitors' innovative ideas. Her natural creativity combined with a taste for disruption may well make her astute at spotting the early fruit of similar talents elsewhere. Ironically, using Molotov's disruptive skills against competitors turns her disruption at home into useful defence.

Will Molotov work well in teams? Seems unlikely given the direction teams often chart towards consensus and away from conflict. But if her manager's training includes consideration of the human ecology that needs to surround Molotov, then yes, she can work effectively in a team.

You are giving a dinner party next week and inviting a great storyteller. So, if one's a good idea, why not invite two raconteurs? You know why not: they'll both be sulking when not fighting for airtime. No, criminally unwise; one is enough. And the same is true for Molotov on a team; she's clear about the revolution she's hatching, and any alternatives will be read as signs of counter-revolutionary dissent. A maximum of one Molotov per team is prudent.

Is Molotov therefore the natural leader of the team? No. Just as the great storyteller at your dinner is not the host, so Molotov is not the team-leader. You, as host, manage the dinner, and the team's leadership must go to someone who, whilst agreeing Molotov's public goals, has pragmatic and diplomatic skills of which Molotov is probably incapable and will certainly scorn. Incidentally, skills similar to those you will use when planning and executing your dinner party.

Molotov's creativity is useful to your company but comes at the price of ensuring her managers understand that its roots lie in her instinctively disruptive attitude to established practices. This is the energy that drives her. All creativity is about change. Molotov isn't excited by the brand that works through graceful evolution, she waves the flag for change *now*.

DEFINITIONS AND CHARACTERISTICS

A colleague is chatting to you at work. "Hey, listen to this! I've just had a really good idea for a new way of getting more clients: we should do…(x)… and that will get them to do…(y)… What do you think, creative eh?" (We can assume she fills in x and y plausibly.) "Right," you reply: "I'll just nip back to my office for a dictionary and check whether what you've just said matches its definition of creativity. I'll let you know."

Definitions of creativity seem little used; both surprising and unsurprising. Surprising in you'd expect companies that rely on creativity would want to know what it actually is; unsurprising in that dictionary definitions aren't really very helpful.

This chapter discusses definitions of creativity, drawing from them two key starting points – but only starting points – for recognising creativity: 'new' and 'useful'. But it also recommends that recognising the characteristics often seen in creative colleagues can be helpful in actually working with them.

Sounds good? No not really, for in that last paragraph I've slipped in some really poor logic, saying that it's useful to recognise characteristics of creative people having just asserted that definitions of creativity are, at best, only marginally helpful. So how do you recognise the person whose characteristics are worth noting? A schoolboy error, but semi-deliberate, for it points with a determined finger towards one of the key 'take-aways' from this chapter: your subjective judgements are key to evaluating creativity. So the correct, but laborious, wording of paragraph three should have been: This chapter discusses definitions of creativity, drawing from them two key starting points – but only starting points – for recognising creativity: 'new' and 'useful'. But it also suggests that recognising the characteristics often seen in colleagues judged as 'creative' by those whose opinions you respect – and that might just be you – can be helpful in actually working with them.

There are many definitions of creativity. Below are just a few.

- 'Creativity is a phenomenon whereby something new and valuable is formed… ' (en.wikipedia.org/wiki/creativity)

- 'Creativity is a process involving the generation of new ideas or concepts, or new associations between existing ideas or concepts, and their substantiation into a product that has novelty and originality.' (newworldencyclopedia.org/entry/creativity)

- 'Creativity is the execution of an idea which has both originality and value.' (https://www.ideatovalue.com/crea/nickskillicorn/2021/05/what-is-creativity-the-definition-history-and-science-of-creativity/)

- 'Creativity, the ability to make or otherwise bring into existence something new, whether a new solution to a problem, a new method or device, or a new artistic object or form.' (britannica.com/topic/creativity)

- 'Creativity is typically defined as the ability to generate novel associations that are adaptive in some way.' (Ward, Thompson Lake, Ely & Kaminski 2008)

- 'Creativity is defined as the production of novel and appropriate ideas.' (Amabile & Conti 1997)

- 'Creativity is one of the words in the English language which means many things to many people.' (Anwar, Shamim-ur-Rasool and Haq 2012)

For the purposes of this chapter, it's simply necessary to note some of the common words that appear in such definitions. These include 'new' and 'useful', or near synonyms such as 'novel' and 'valuable'. So far so good: a fairly consistent definition seems to be emerging. But those apparently key words sometimes appear as modifiers to others. So we sometimes read phrases such as 'new associations between existing ideas' and 'the ability to generate novel associations'.

To my mind, 'associations' is a process-related word and, although preceded by the keyword 'new', inches the sentence away from defining what creativity is, to describing how it does it; a characteristic rather than a definition of creativity. I can see that many might argue that 'creativity', being a process itself, could well insist that such an important, and perhaps universal, element of that process must appear in its definition, but I'm not entirely convinced; is it perhaps unhelpful in a definition but a useful hint about the value of recognising the characteristics of creativity?

Anyway, you might find that bit of speculation interesting or terminally dull, and it's fine; whichever you choose won't affect your ability to work with or manage your creative colleagues. Those, however, who find it all rather fascinating, should look at Panagiotis Kampylis' article in *The Journal of Creative Behavior* entitled Redefining Creativity – Analyzing Definitions, Collocations, and Consequences (see *Sources cited*).

Words with meanings distant from 'new' and 'useful' also appear from time to time in definitions of creativity. The one offered by the *Encyclopaedia Britannica* given above includes 'a new solution to a problem, a new method or device, or a new artistic object or form.' But to my mind these start to get dangerously close to falling down the rabbit hole of specificity, in feeling obliged to start listing things upon which creativity can be exercised. A comprehensive list of the objects of creativity would require more than the word count of the whole *Encyclopaedia Britannica*, and anything other than a complete list would prompt screams of: "Outrageous, what about... you've missed it out!" Best to forget lists and keep definitions general.

So, I conclude that there is a rough and ready consensus that creativity has simply to be 'new' and 'useful' – or words that mean much the same. The road seems clear ahead, for this book suggests ways in which you can interact positively with your creative colleagues at work, and now you know how to recognise them: they are the ones doing the new and useful stuff.

You are up and running in your search for the creatives! If only that were true, for how do you recognise newness and usefulness? And I'm afraid my use of the word 'you' in that last sentence, rather than the more scholarly 'one', is not a result of my oddly informal literary tone, but a simple statement of fact; for the choice of criteria used to recognise newness and usefulness is entirely down to You.

Clutching 'new' and 'useful', you might appear to be holding a universal and objective double-lever key to recognising a creative colleague; but all you've really received is a gentle, vague nudge in a sensible direction. You're still a long way from having a reliable sieve through which to process your decision on whether or not your colleague's idea is significantly creative. And that's because both 'new' and 'useful' require buckets of subjective interpretation before you can get to an answer. The answer is itself subjective, being dependent upon your specific knowledge of the context that surrounds you, your colleague, and the big idea. But don't despair, we all do this automatically every day.

Your subjective understanding of context will flesh out both 'newness' and 'usefulness' without much difficulty – often without conscious thought at all – allowing you to decide whether you're really face to face with the product of creativity. Perhaps the idea that is being explained to you by your excited colleague is really new or perhaps just a new application of an existing process; and if the latter, is that new enough? Your knowledge of the context will inform your answer. And it's the same process with your judgement of usefulness. Just how useful does an innovation have to be to pass the creativity test? So, context is again king, but its salient elements are yours and only yours to identify. Perhaps they'll include the degree to which competent craft skills have been energised by a new insight; perhaps you recognise that the colleague's apparently new product is but a thinly disguised recycling of a competitor's creativity – fine to go ahead and market it, but not an indicator of your colleague's significant creativity.

No-one is likely to understand the context of possible work-based 'newness' or 'usefulness' better than a colleague or manager. Your subjective nose for creativity is much more sensitive than that of any lexicographer and relieves me of the duty to propose yet another definition of creativity.

Do you recall the imaginary conversation you had with your colleague at the start of this chapter, the one that had you scurrying off to your dictionary in order to test whether your colleague's new idea was 'creative'? Ludicrous: all that the dictionary definition of 'creativity' could have done is suggest you ask your colleague about the novelty and utility of her idea, and then the judgement would be up to you.

If you can be bothered, your computer's search engine will

quickly offer many more definitions of creativity. Hidden among them you'll sometimes spot, not a definition of creativity, but a description of creative people. One of my favourites comes from the distinguished American psychologist and philosopher, Frank Barron. *The creative person is both more primitive and more cultivated, more destructive, a lot madder and a lot saner, than the average person.*

Two things appeal to me in this description. First, the internal contradictions make it obviously and utterly unusable as a reliable objective sieve for recognising creative people, correctly placing the responsibility firmly on the subjective shoulders of the courageous person wishing to make this judgement. The second reason why I like the description is that it presents a mixed-up, contradictory picture of extremes, and this, to my subjective mind, accurately echoes the often confused process of being creative.

Barron shifts his focus away from defining creativity to describing some features of creative people. I do the same in this book. My fictional caricatures – Picky, Solo, Artiste, Wobbly etc. – attempt to describe characteristics of creative people but do not define creativity itself. Perhaps more importantly, my caricatures offer some disentangling of the contradictions central to Barron's overall picture of the creative person. I do this by isolating groups of broadly cognate and distinctive characteristics and assigning them to a singular name that encapsulates that region of creativity. In this way, the daunting mass of conflicting and contradictory characteristics noted (accurately) in Barron's broad-brush approach can be painted more finely and coherently, at the expense, I regret, of his dramatic landscape.

I discuss in the introduction to this book the temptation to read my caricatures as real people, or conversely, to read real people as living embodiments of one-dimensional characteristics. Here, it's enough to suggest that a manager may well see certain behaviours in his or her creative colleagues reminiscent of the essences distilled in one or more of my caricatures. And, having understood through my analysis of the caricature how best to interact with that behaviour, the manager will be able to facilitate a colleague's creativity.

One final similarity between Barron's and my process of considering creative people: neither of us is offering a sieve. I've already discussed the limits of attempting to use definitions of creativity as an apparently objective sieve for identifying significantly creative people. I'm now warning against a similarly tempting and equally unwise use of Barron's broad description and my detailed caricatures. Barron suggests that the creative person is more destructive than the average person. Maybe; seems likely to me. But what he is definitely not suggesting is that an individual's destructive tendency is a marker for creativity. It's not a sieve to be used for identifying creativity. In the same way, it is commonly recognised that many creative people produce their best work when left alone; I call the caricature that crystallises this tendency 'Solo'. Through this I'm not suggesting that everybody who prefers working alone does so for the sake of their creativity.

SUMMARY

- Existing definitions of creativity are helpful only to the extent of having articulated a consensual view that originality and utility are present in products of humanity generally judged significantly creative.

- The telescope of definition should not however be reversed using the search words 'originality' and 'utility' to judge the work of an apparently creative colleague without a deep understanding of the many contexts that surround and inform that colleague's work.

- Although still not an objective creative-spotting device, understanding and recognising the common characteristics displayed at work by significantly creative colleagues will assist managers and colleagues in nurturing the degree of creativity available.

ARTISTE

"IT'S NOT THAT I'M PROUD OF MY WORK, JUST THAT I
UNDERSTAND ITS VALUE."

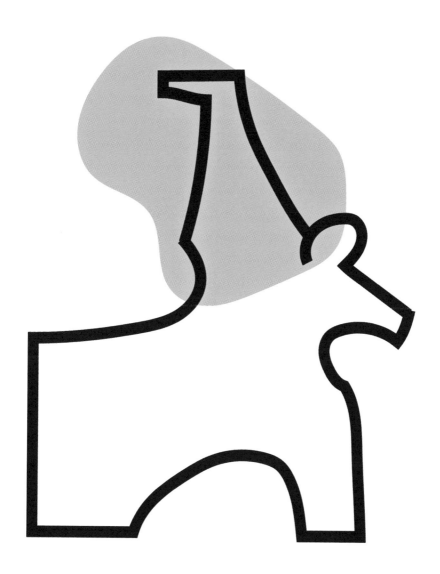

Artiste is your somewhat precious colleague and you are her manager. She's creative and produces good work that helps the innovative drive of your company. Oh, but you so wish she were easier to work with!

'The main problem with Artiste is she just can't take criticism – even the most constructive. Her face just creases up and I know she's turned off her audio input. And my comments weren't insensitive or wounding. So why?

'She's actually rather good in teams and enjoys talking about her latest project as long as it's being praised. Not good at hearing, and certainly not taking, advice though.

'Artiste hates watching focus groups and gets really twitchy when they're judging her work. But when its complimented she's a different person. I'd swear she actually glows! I know everybody likes that reaction, but for Artiste it's as if her life depends on it, a sort of oxygen for her.

'And there's one final thing about Artiste: she can't let a project go. Even after she's done all the initial creative stuff, and the implementation people are working out the nuts and bolts, she still demands to be involved. It's now way beyond her skill set. She should let it go and get on with the next creative project, but she just can't.'

So that's what you, her fictional manager, might think of Artiste. But have you met her in your real-life company? Or perhaps beyond your organisation? The primary school gate is a likely place. Here you'll see parents bristling at any criticism of their children, and beatifically smiling if another parent compliments them on what a lovely child they have. There will be parents itching to talk about their child's latest achievement and eager to escort him or her right into the classroom despite the school's plea to say goodbye at the gate.

Artiste at work/parent at school gate: resenting criticism; desperate for praise; eager to display; and reluctant to let go. Artiste's work is her child, the tangible expression of her own creative DNA. No surprise then that she should guard, nurture and promote it in the way she does. But how might this understanding help you as her manager?

Unfortunately, the obvious way forward is probably not available to you, for treating her as you would another parent at the school gate is impractical. You cannot reconcile the needs of your company with the parental tactic of: say nothing critical to another parent; just smile and listen to their stories; and agree it's a silly rule about saying goodbye at the school gate. No, your company's legitimate needs of quality, commercial viability, timescales and efficiency mean that you, the manager, must be more assertive than you, the parent. But remembering, as you roll up your sleeves, that you're working with a person deeply in love with the fragile and vulnerable idea she has just delivered, will guide you in your management of Artiste.

I know an Artiste. She works in dance, an art form within which teamwork is key to creativity. About her work she is justifiably defensive or unbelievably precious, depending on whether you're Artiste or a colleague of Artiste. In line with my description of Artistes generally, my particular Artiste protects her work, understanding suggestions as hostile takeover bids. She seems, however, unusually pragmatic about evaluation, simply shrugging her shoulders and moving on, rather than seeing it as an attack. This interests me, for, unwounded, she simply continues in the direction she was anyway taking; evaluation seldom alters her course. My earlier description showed Artistes in general abreacting strongly against perceived criticism within evaluation; my Artiste follows this pattern but has the luxury of simply ignoring the evaluation and searching for her next role.

I wonder therefore if there is something narcissistic about Artistes. I'm not qualified to judge the psychology of this, but surely a creative person in love with the products of her creation, to the extent that they become barriers to self-development, possesses an unhealthy predisposition?

One symptom of many Artistes' heightened self-regard is a tendency to overvalue loyalty, both professional and personal. This is, I suppose, predictable for they must, in a sense, surround themselves with uncritical supporters if their equilibrium is to be sustained. The colleague who considers that his historic support of an Artiste has earned him the right to comment negatively on a later aspect of her work had better look out: betrayal is a crime.

More positively, Artiste's immovable belief in her own creativity gives her indomitable determination to achieve her goals. She is never nudged off-course, forced to compromise her vision or replace her own goals with those of others. Whether this tunnel vision is in others' best interests or even her own is, of course, dependent on the creative quality of what she mines from her chosen tunnel.

I once asked my dancing Artiste how she coped with working on team projects – and being a dancer she should know. Her reply was revealing: "I just get on with my bit of it." And that's the obvious way any Artiste will probably learn to handle their form of creativity: avoid contact and thus possible contamination by others as far as possible unless they are consistent and unfailing fans.

But what if the opportunity to 'just get on with my bit of it' ends; perhaps the show closes or the design department moves to other incompatible projects. What does Artiste do then? There are two classic answers that creatives in general give in this almost inevitable situation. Most will just roll up their peripatetic creativity and carry it with them to the next object on which they can practice it. So, the designer shifts from designing domestic washing machines to dryer technology, the lawyer to politics, the journalist to novels, the architect to web design. Most creatives wisely see their ability to create as separate from the medium in which they currently create. As long as they possess sufficient craft skills in the new medium, their innate creativity is transferrable. A few creatives do not, however, take this divergent, and to my mind insightful, view, choosing instead to see their creativity as inseparable from the particular ambition they are pursuing. Artiste is in this smaller group; Monk, often another. The result for Artiste is that she would rather 'fill-in' with some tedious and mundane job whilst searching for the role that is designed perfectly for her, than look elsewhere for a workable vehicle through which she can express her undoubted creativity.

I've described one Artiste I know, the dancer, but there is another: I'll call her V. Artiste – and indeed she was! She expressed her defensiveness in a way rather different to my first Artiste, for V. Artiste worked permanently in a department of an organisation and so didn't use the transportable nature of her creativity in the way that the dancer did. Instead, she created a comfortable castle for herself inside a defensive wall around her empire. And it wasn't just a protection to keep others out, but a statement that everything needed by those in her orbit was contained within its walls. V. Artiste was the benevolent empress and her subjects loved her.

The problem was that her subjects' own creativity was clearly tending towards that of V. Artiste's own. Their creative ideas were being constrained by the lack of diversity within the empire and by a desire to conform to the processes and goals of their empress. Additionally, these dangers might have been exacerbated by V. Artiste's powers of patronage, which her subjects were understandably reluctant to put at risk. But what really surprised me was the enthusiasm with which most of her creative colleagues welcomed their apprenticeship as mini-V. Artistes! Some rebelled, but this was dangerous given V. Artiste's primacy.

The studios of many Old Master painters operated in a similar way, so much so that the later products of the apprentices can often be confused with the work of the Master himself. It seems to me a pity when the honest acquisition of craft skills drifts into the stifling of originality.

Five ideas for working with Artiste

- Being a good colleague to Artiste is usually harder than being her manager. A colleague may have to choose to be either her apparently unquestioning fan or her distant and probably disliked associate. Her manager, with the wisdom to understand Artiste's attitude to her own creativity, will be able to ensure as far as possible, that Artiste can simply 'just get on with her bit of the job'. When this isn't possible, a manager might protect colleagues from Artiste's anger by delivering all evaluation him- or herself. The manager should however loudly celebrate Artiste's creative successes, which, because of her limitless dedication, may well be significant.

- Would it be wise if the manager were to prise apart Artiste's possibly narcissistic defensiveness and aggression from her creativity? Probably not. Artiste's manager is almost certainly unqualified for such a specialist psychological task, and unless Artiste herself decides this action would be positive for her, external intervention will probably be angrily rejected.

- Before facilitating any structured review of Artiste's work, the wise manager will arrange a one-to-one coffee with Artiste. The manager should start with some self-criticism of a project he or she is currently working on, a project nothing to do with Artiste, but on which she may well wish to comment. (Parent readers will here recognise the 'Coffee after drop-off and my child's a real worry at the moment' tactic to encourage another parent to open-up.)

- Delay formal criticism of Artiste's work until it's strong enough to take it. This in practice may mean a lengthened period between the birth of Artiste's idea and its first public outing in front of peers. When this does eventually take place, avoid both a focus group with its tendency to premature conclusions and groupthink, as well as brainstorming Artiste's idea in potentially brutal competition with others. A more low-key Artiste-led SWOT analysis might be more useful. (Chapter 16 *Creatives and evaluation* discusses in detail how and when to give critical feedback to creative colleagues.)

- After Artiste's work on the project has ended, facilitate her keeping in touch with its progress out in the commercial world. This might include her being informed of results it's generating, and could also prompt her being invited – for comments only – to review meetings discussing modifications in its deployment.

Your company hired Artiste for her creativity not her easy management. As her manager, you agree she can be frustrating. At the same time, you can't help but sympathise with, even respect, her attitude to her work. Perhaps you're a bit Artiste; there are a lot of us about.

CREATIVES, THEIR MANAGERS AND THEIR COLLEAGUES

This chapter discusses the blurred distinction between the manager and the colleague of a creative employee. It does this by trying to notate the sometimes surprising choreography they both perform around a creative person. It is not the business of this chapter to describe – even less explain – the reasons they take the steps they do, this is the job of later chapters. It is, however, important in a book about creatives and these two groups of people who work with them, to get an early but moderately clear view of who they are and the basic shapes of the dances they perform.

The chapter's overall conclusion is that the successful manager of a creative person will probably be seen to adopt patterns of interaction with the creative, significantly closer to that usually seen among same-level colleague to colleague relationships; interactions which certainly breach more usual, hierarchical, manager-to-managed convention. It also suggests that a fruitful junction between the creative and his or her creative colleague – regardless of respective levels – is likely to display some characteristics of traditional management style that I've just suggested the wise manager will be putting to one side. All a bit skew whiff. The dance doesn't exactly swap the roles of manager and colleague, but you could be forgiven when viewing it from the bar, that with all its movement, it's not always clear which is which. But let's start with some solid introductions…

When referring to the creative's manager, I'm talking about
an employee who has direct responsibility for the work of
the creative, rather than enjoying a more senior and distanced
level of authority. She may or may not be significantly creative
herself. When discussing the creative's colleagues, I'm including
all employees with close working relationships with, but no
managerial responsibility for, the creative; perhaps fulfilling
creative functions themselves, perhaps not.

The creative's manager has a tough job, one for which normal
diligence is a disadvantage, even dangerous. The familiar tools
of good management such as regular review meetings to judge
progress and quality of work against timelines and budgets
are likely to be instruments of torture, not necessarily to the
creative himself but to the quality of output he is working hard
to produce. The detailed reasons for this are given in Chapter
10 *Creatives, deadlines and teams* and in Chapter 16 *Creatives and
evaluation*. Sufficient, here, simply to assert that timelines, budgets
and premature evaluation are all precisely destructive of the
indeterminate, divergent and deliciously unpredictable restaurant
in which creativity, above that of simple problem-solving, gets its
nourishment and myriad flavours.

So, the effective manager of the creative holds back from
tugging on normal levers of line management and instead, after
a commendably clear, but empty project brief (see Chapter 20

Project briefs, task allocation and diverse non-conformists) steps back in an apparently indolent fashion. The manager, if not particularly creative herself, may feel guilty at this, but should be reassured it's fine, and an easily learned technique that is necessary if significant creativity is perhaps to emerge. In this way we see the manager consciously abjuring a traditional managerial stance and appearing more like an interested colleague of the creative with no formal authority over him.

If the manager is herself creative, she is more likely – but not certain – to be happy with this hands-off attitude. 'Likely' because she will have experienced herself the need to be left alone in this way and will consequently appreciate that her colleague's creativity must be treated with the same respect. But this is not certain, for she may not understand how her own creativity works to the degree necessary to externalise its principles for the benefit of other creatives. She might therefore, mystified, grab nervously for conventional, but inappropriate, levers of encouragement and control.

And, I'm afraid, this manager is easy prey to another lethal temptation that her less creative manager-counterpart is likely to avoid: "Hey, that looks fun! I could really help with that bit of creativity. Hang on mate I've got some really great ideas, you'll love 'em!" The creative's manager must not invade, it will simply compromise the quality of the creative's work, exactly the opposite of what the manager is trying to achieve. Chapter 13 *Facilitator* presents a theory supporting this counter-intuitive conclusion. Again, by declining to 'step-in' or 'direct', the wise manager is appearing more like a colleague of the creative than his traditional manager.

So, what's left for the manager; does she actually have anything left to do? Yes; in summary, her job is to protect the creative from the bureaucracy of the company, ensure he has sufficient resources, and translate – both ways – between organisation-speak and creative-speak. Again, Chapter 13 *Facilitator* gives details on these vital and difficult, managerial duties.

Now to the creative's colleagues whom I suggested might be adopting some characteristics from the traditional manager's repertoire. Colleagues can risk questioning and criticising a creative's work to a much higher degree than can the manager. I have explained why she has to hold back, but the creative's colleagues have no formal authority over his work, and this is known both by them and the creative. The creative does not therefore read colleagues' interest as a challenge or as a command to leave the creative process. The colleagues' criticism is therefore far less invasive than that of the manager, for their interest doesn't carry real weight or pretend to have the subject knowledge and experience of the manager. Additionally, normal colleague criticism is generally conducted in a perfectly healthy bantering/joshing manner that comes with none of the evaluative implications of a manager using the same words.

Colleagues who are also creative themselves will probably be able to empathise with the traumatic process of incubating a deeply creative idea and so will certainly be of more quasi-managerial assistance – if only from informed sympathy – than will the real manager if not significantly creative herself.

From these examples it can be seen that empathic or well-trained colleagues of creatives can, from time to time, seem to pick up some of the discarded tokens of the manager.

Sometimes however, an evolving relationship with a creative colleague may be rather more than tokenistic. I've sometimes observed a team of colleagues, all working on the same project, becoming increasingly concerned that the creative among them seems increasingly unlikely to deliver his – often initial stage – output in a form or at a date convenient for them to add their inputs. A rather embarrassing example of this occurred when I was asked to compose some incidental music for a production of a play by W. B. Yeats. The request came very late and I was unable to complete the work before rehearsals started, rehearsals that should have decided how my music was to be incorporated into the show. After a few postponements, designed to allow me to catch-up, the director – wisely – decided that the play didn't really need any music after all. Relief all round. But I, the show's director, and W. B. Yeats had been lucky, my failed contribution was always just a nice-to-have 'extra'.

But what if a creative's contribution is fundamental to the project? In such a situation, the problem is serious and the project team's normally unchallenging interest in their creative's work can become incisive and thus potentially injurious to the creative's sense of security. The manager should handle this carefully, addressing the legitimate concerns of the creative's colleagues whilst, as far as possible, ensuring that the quality of the creative's work is protected. The manager, in this situation, should be used as a skilful go-between.

In conclusion, the manager and the creative's colleagues seem ideally to morph in and out of traditional manager and colleague roles, forming a flexible knowledge base for the creative to use in the early 'incubation' stage of creativity in which initial information is randomly processed. They then circle the creative as a tolerant and protective team of supporters watching over the emergence of his creativity.

So, colleague or manager, it often really doesn't make much difference to the creative, and the careful reader of this book will frequently notice times when I've presented ideas valuable to both (or neither). Their interchangeability should however serve to remind senior managers in organisations which rely on creativity, to make sure all employees, be they managers or colleagues, understand the principles of the creative process and how to look after it.

PLAYFUL

"IF YOU CAN'T HAVE A BIT OF FUN AT WORK, WHAT'S THE POINT?"

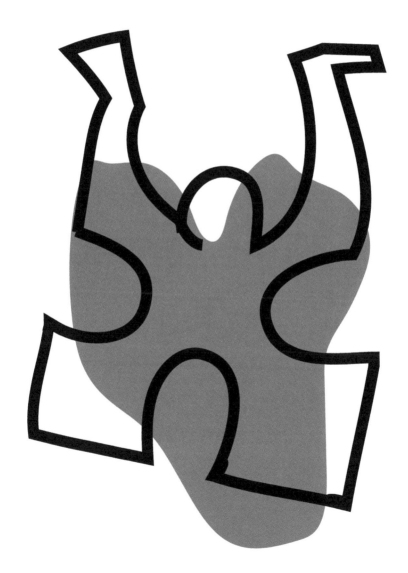

Have you got any annoying colleagues at work; yes? But is there one who sticks out? So irritating, but at other times really fun to work with? Odd, your mind is pretty much made up about the others, but with this guy? Just can't figure it. Sometimes he's a real pain: forgetting about that key meeting; missing the deadline; coming up with ideas totally off the point; sulks; even tantrums! But then his enthusiasm, the sheer joy of his working practice and the originality and fun of his creative ideas draw you into his world, a world closer to the school playground than the office coffee machine. His name's Playful. Know him?

Time, ambition and optimism are often found at the roots of creativity. Do you have all three? I certainly don't; time is definitely absent, middle age makes that almost inevitable, and by old age I expect I'll be crossing off 'optimism' too. So, the only stage of life when these three conditions stand a decent chance of being present is childhood: time to play; dream; and just know those dreams can be achieved. Playful, although middle-aged and working in a big organisation, has kept a door open to his childhood, and it's on the other side of that door that all his most creative ideas germinate.

There he spots novel associations among ideas, emotions and dreams within a diverse world where everything is a pregnant possibility waiting to emerge. It may look like chaos to us, who have forgotten the thrill of the place, but to Playful – who has never totally left childhood – it's a sphere seething with life and demanding his creative alchemy. With luck, he returns through the door to our grown-up world clutching an idea with an almost magical genesis.

I wonder if our irritation at his childlike workday characteristics is genuine annoyance or rather jealousy. And perhaps the occasions when we find him delightful are when the door to his own childhood remains sufficiently open for us to glimpse our own, when we too had oodles of time, ambition and optimism. Maybe.

The positive column of Playful's attributes at work is reassuringly long. Not only does he often come up with stunningly novel ideas, but he also shrugs off disappointments and setbacks more easily than most; his eyes already focused on his next adventure. Surprisingly for an apparent anarchist who relishes a divergent environment, Playful respects rules and insists others follow them to the letter; although this is a principle he doesn't always follow himself. As you'd expect, Playful is popular with colleagues, but less so with those with whom he works closely, who can become irritated at his sulks and rapid changes of direction as a more attractive alternative 'game' appears. But he works hard whilst focused on a project and has a tolerant attitude to deadlines; unusual among creatives.

You may notice that Playful's creativity is of a rather different order to that of Artiste. His skittishness and volatile focus dissuade him from taking time slowly to explore and then incubate his creative ideas to the extent that an Artiste or Monk believes necessary. His creativity may be more immediately arresting than theirs, but is less likely to possess such profundity, failing to appreciate that his own zany, off the wall ideas probably need, at some point, to grow-up into coherent and sustainable decisions. He is likely to find this mature process unpalatable or simply boring when compared to the new idea now starting to fire his imagination. This has implications for Playful's manager in choosing the projects or accounts on which Playful will be most useful.

Although he's able to get over professional disappointments quite easily, personal slights – as he perceives them – are harder and can result in distinctly inappropriate meltdowns. Here, he may blame a colleague for refusing to cooperate (play) with him in the way, or to the extent, that he wishes, and then run to his manager complaining that 'it's just not fair!' Playful's wise colleagues will therefore have warned the manager in advance if they need, for professional reasons, to withdraw from close support of Playful for a time.

Could Playful become an effective manager? No: his inconsistency and unnerving volatility almost certainly disqualify him from the role. I suppose if he were able to stand outside himself and understand his own preferred style of working, he might be able to temper it for others and thus learn to manage adequately, but this asks a lot of Playful; if all you've got is a balloon, a ball and a whoopee cushion then everything is a game. Playful the manager might be fun, but only for a very short time.

Playful's manager may well be tempted to try a little amateur psychology on Playful. This is because the manager is more likely to recognise patterns in his behaviour more easily than those of other creatives; this is particularly likely if the manager has lived with children. The temptation to wade in with 'parental' guidance will be strong, but should, I believe, be avoided. The manager should attempt to remain the professional 'adult' in the playroom whose job is to facilitate Playful's commercially valuable creativity, and shield, when and where necessary, Playful's colleagues from his sometimes excessive childish behaviour.

There are a few management options to draw from this crude sketch of Playful's creativity. A manager needs to understand Playful's creative process and resist saying: "JUST GROW UP!", "We're here to work not play…", or, "You've got to learn to take the job more seriously." These are tempting, yet daft instructions to bark at Playful; for his creativity is dependent on his easy access to a childlike condition, and you hired him for his creativity not his skills with the new accounting system or diary management. To attempt to make him 'JUST GROW UP!' will undermine his ability to do what you want him to do.

Okay, so Playful's manager might quite easily learn to adopt an unusually tolerant attitude to his professional behaviour, but what about Playful's colleagues, how can they work happily and effectively with someone whose motivation comes from a source the've probably forgotten ever existed?

I have earlier warned against Playful's manager attempting some amateur psychology by taking on a 'parental' role in response to Playful's child ego state. However, whilst still avoiding amateur psychology, I think it is helpful for his colleagues – who have no managerial responsibility but a personal interest in their interaction with him – to sometimes deploy, in self-defence, some parental tactics without stepping beyond professional propriety.

When Playful wants a playmate, the parental: "No, I'm sorry darling, I really haven't time to play right now…" could be work-translated into: "No way, got to finish this wretched report!" And the parent's: "Haven't you got some homework?" becomes: "I really do need that bit of work from you asap so I can add my bit." Playful's colleagues should understand his unusual ways of working, but nevertheless ensure their own preferred styles are protected through interactions that may be more assertive and unambiguous than those usually voiced with colleagues. Playful's child-like disposition may well require and accept this more peremptory tone.

Working in a team with Playful can be problematical. Teams often base their innovations on evolution, so Playful's apparently intuitive methods will seem disconcertingly spontaneous to them, whilst their frequent search for consensus and practicality will sit uncomfortably with Playful's more anarchic creative process. So, Playful's manager should scaffold his involvement in teams, ensuring his ideas are heard early and carried forward to pragmatic outcomes without his continuing involvement.

Fortunately, few Playfuls will object to being relieved of 'all that boring stuff'.

Good training is key to working with Playful, and that's training for his managers and colleagues rather than training for Playful himself. The wise organisation will conclude that attempting to chisel Playful out of his preferred way of working is pointless and contrary to the best interests of the company. Just let him get on with his own innovative work in his own way and help his managers and colleagues to accommodate his unique contribution whilst enjoying the fruits of his creativity.

WHY DO I DO WHAT I DO?

Do you play football? Perhaps tennis, maybe badminton? Or is it jogging or dancing for you? Why… why do you do it?

'To get a bit fitter' – that's extrinsic motivation.

'Because I love the game' – intrinsic.

'To earn a living' – extrinsic.

'It's just so beautiful' – intrinsic.

'I like showing I'm quite good at it' – extrinsic.

'I haven't a clue why. I just have to do it' – intrinsic.

Consider this fictional little story:

You are an engineer designing components of jet engines. Your current project is optimising the power to fuel ratio of the engine by redesigning two key interacting elements. You enjoy your job. One evening at home, whilst relaxing with a glass of wine and flicking through a trashy 'make your home beautiful' magazine, you notice an advert for a new vacuum cleaner. Perhaps it caught your eye because your partner had said a couple of days earlier that your own vacuum was making funny noises, or maybe it was that random dream last night? Maybe it was just accidental, who knows; who cares? Anyway, this advertisement was trying to sound scientifically impressive and mentioned a new metal alloy that it claimed gave the cleaner more suck: 'More suck for your buck'. You weren't impressed, but simply curious. So, the next evening after a perfectly average day at work, during which you tested adjusting the width of one of your key fuel/power components, you looked up some respectable online journals on metallurgy and found out what this new alloy really was. It turned out to have some remarkable heat dissipating qualities; perhaps useful in jet engines too? Your curiosity now turned to excitement. Okay, it was nothing to do with power to fuel ratios, but maybe useful to other aspects of jet engines? The next day at work you decide to do a bit of further work researching the new alloy. You don't yet chat to colleagues about it, but after a few days you go to see your manager and suggest she might want to have a preliminary look at possibilities. Your manager agrees and sets up an informal working group. But alloys aren't really your area of expertise or even interest, and it'll be detailed work from this point, so you decline her invitation to join the team and you go happily back to your day-job of power to fuel ratios and those two, bothersome but key, interacting components. Lots more adjustments to try, but you'll get there in the end! It's just a case of trying one adjustment after another…

What motivated you to act in the way you did?

Your interest was generated by the investigative process itself: your sense of personal involvement in it; your curiosity; personal satisfaction; and thirst for challenge. These, broadly speaking, are intrinsic motivators. Your motivation was certainly not at the extrinsic end of the motivation spectrum. You clearly did not embark on your little side-project for financial reward or reputational gain, positive professional evaluation, promotion or that 'employee of the month' award.

No, your motivation for resisting turning to the next page of your magazine came from your own creative curiosity rather than from a tactical calculation of potential external advantage. Circumstantial evidence for this overwhelmingly intrinsic motivation: the subject of your curiosity was not part of your official job; your creative idea came whilst you were away from your place of work; and you turned down the offer to continue the investigation, probably because the creative 'I wonder if...' stage was now about to evolve into a more instrumental and pragmatic stage, laden with extrinsic motivations. You relished the abstract tune forming in your head and had no enthusiasm for its mechanical instrumentation.

Motivation necessary for higher level creativity tends to be intrinsic, whilst extrinsic motivation can restrict creativity by encouraging a researcher to abort the sometimes arduous, prolonged and uncertain search for profound creativity once the extrinsic reward is secured. You pursued your interest in the metal alloy for its own sake, not for any extrinsic payoff, and not for the possible instrumental utility of your creativity. Indeed, you left the project at the point at which your abstract creativity was about to morph into instrumental pragmatism. Highly creative people tend to be engrossed in projects for their own sake rather than for tangible results which may follow, and this engrossment is nurtured by intrinsic motivation and handicapped by extrinsic rewards. And yet, what are some common levers used today to motivate colleagues? Pay-rise, promotions, car parking space, status, title, posher office, gym membership… All extrinsic motivators; all injurious to higher-level creativity.

I'm told that Leonardo Da Vinci often irritated his patrons by being slow at completing his artistic commissions, or, on too many occasions, by not completing them at all. I wonder if he was like 'you' with the new alloy: the intrinsically thrilling conceptual and creative stage was ending; the next demanded pragmatism with the poisonous lure of extrinsic reward. Best stop now and instead move on to another creative challenge.

Returning to 'make your home beautiful', the period between your seeing the advertisement for the vacuum cleaner and sharing your idea with your manager, would, I suspect, be described by the great creativity expert, Teresa Amabile, as time valuably spent in the Creative Maze (See *Sources cited* Amabile, T. 1996).

Amabile's 'maze' is an imaginary zone within which creativity is born. It is tantalisingly difficult to talk about without using metaphors, each of which dangerously trails its own, often misleading, associations. So let me start to describe it by simply listing some possible reactions of creative people who have just emerged from it. All were asked to come up with an idea for a new product their companies could manufacture. All have achieved that goal, but they emerge from different exits of the maze: the first appears from exit one; the second, from exit three;

and the last from exit five. Listen to their thoughts:

Exit 1: "Yeah, an okay idea, it'll do. At least I've made the deadline – that'll keep my boss happy. It's a satisfactory idea, they won't sack me for coming up with that. Easy to come up with. Quick too. Plenty of time for lunch; where shall I go today?"

Exit 3: "Yeah good, and Marketing should like it as well as my manager. I was thinking about Marketing as I planned it – that really helped. Could be a bit over budget though; but it's worth it, and so much better than our competitors' products or the work of that creepy new guy in the next cubicle. Yeah, good, well done! Hard work but worth it. A glass of wine with lunch today. I deserve it!"

Exit 5: "Great idea! So exciting, and I just loved feeling it kind of emerge in my mind. Difficult to get it though, and took a long time but soooo satisfying! Skipping lunch today – I want to think a bit more about my new idea."

So the maze is a metaphorical zone Amabile has built to describe some aspects of human creativity. My crude 'exit comments' illustrate that a creative person is likely to bring his or her own professional and personal context into the maze, and that this will influence the quality of creativity there incubated.

Of the three colleagues, the one at exit five clearly has the best chance of leaving with the most creative idea. It has been prompted by the intrinsic pleasure and excitement of creativity

itself, rather than the constraints of extrinsic motivators.
The other two creatives – the first particularly strongly – were
more concerned with extrinsic motivators such as: time and cost
constraints; the judgement of the boss; competition from inside
and beyond the company; and concerns about the practicality of
the idea.

The creative maze does not therefore guarantee a particular level
of creativity but is sensitive to the contexts that surround the
creative person entering it.

Amabile's array of five exits to the maze is, to my mind, a
helpfully graphic way of illustrating the spectrum of creativity
– from banal problem solving to profound innovation – that
humans can achieve. My three colleagues exemplify how
increasing susceptibility to extrinsic motivators predicts inferior
creativity depicted by the lower numbered exits of the maze.

Now let's extend the metaphorical language of the maze a little
further by adding 'time' and 'effort'. You'll notice that our exit
one colleague reported his work in the maze was 'easy and quick'
whilst that from exit three reported 'hard work but worth it', and,
from exit five, that the creative idea was 'difficult to get… and
took a long time'. So the maze seems to posses the dimensions
of time and effort as well as 'space'. This is helpful for it allows
us to use these familiar words to picture some far more illusive
processes: physical; mental; psycho-social; spiritual; that humans
may actually employ whilst creating.

Time and effort exist both inside the maze and in the real-world of the three creative people I've sketched. Indeed, but time and effort as understood within the maze should be kept distinct from real time and real effort beyond the maze. Within the maze profound creativity presupposes time and effort devoted to exploring its furthest reaches. Outside, that same creative person might simply experience an immeasurably short moment of apparently inevitable insight, or, equally plausibly, months, years of dedicated hard labour.

So, what is the human experience of exploring the maze? Surely, the subject of an entire library of books, a different one for every creative person, or perhaps even for each creative moment of each creative person? All I can report is my own experience of the rare occasions when I risk something a bit beyond solving my next problem.

My maze is a mess. A total mess of random ideas, memories, sounds, pictures… Even to label them as diverse, contradictory or confusing pretends a degree of classification that doesn't exist. And in this mess I just wander aimlessly about, aware of the stuff I'm wading though, watching, listening, but with no aim or sense of direction, discovery or fun. It's actually all a bit of a chore really. But then – and this always happens – a few bits of detritus I'm forcing my way through sort of clump together as if they've got something in common. Then another pair recognise each other and sometimes this pair will relate in some way to the first pair. Perhaps they agree, perhaps together they point to another bit of rubbish over there. It might be interesting: go and look. Eventually the clumping of memories, ideas and pictures start to form a canyon revealing what might become a path through the rubbish tip. There are no magical transformations of rubbish into new valuable creations, but simply the start of a possible direction in which I might go. But I'm not the passive recipient of all this, I sense no destiny. I still have my brain, so I weigh up the various possible directions emerging, totally free to reject them as a waste of time, illogical or banal. There's more rubbish to be kicked about.

Eventually (that's maze 'eventually'; in real-life it might have been a nano-second) a path I respect appears, and that's where I'm going. This, for me, is the creative moment in which I know what I'm doing and am confident I can do it. The maze now turns itself into the most complete library imaginable and I wander around its shelves, no longer aimlessly, but pulling out ideas, testing them against one another, forming, reforming and deforming hypotheses, playing with contradictions, juggling possibilities. All such fun, plotting my path, refining my idea, proud of what I'm creating. Polishing, highlighting.

Right, time to leave the maze. But I don't feel that it is I who leaves it. More that the maze sort of evaporates from around me having finished looking after me. It can now gradually withdraw, I know who and what I am, and that certainty is crystallised in the idea now cradled in my mind. Time now for bit of pragmatism: getting it actually to work! Boring, it was much more fun in there.

But that's just my maze; what's yours like?

Persisting in the maze until an idea worthy of exits four or five often requires significant creative energy. Why would your colleague devote that much effort to the company's success when exit three is probably good enough? One reason, beyond the fun and excitement of the maze itself, may be because he or she shares, or at least respects, the values of your company.

Effective values reach out from the boardroom to all employees creating trust and a shared sense of commitment. If these values are humane and aspirational, rather than mechanical and mercenary, they are likely to attract the support of creative colleagues (Chapter 15 *Monk* suggests reasons why this is generally the case). And if the creatives feel this trust in their organisation's direction, they will be willing to work for exit five of the maze; for it's worth the major investment of effort and personal involvement. Or, put the other way round: 'Why would I put my heart and soul – as well as my brain – into an organisation that doesn't have values I share?'

To get high-end (exit five) ideas from creatives, organisations must offer more than just the normal contract with colleagues: extrinsic rewards of salary, promotion and perhaps a car parking space in return for employee competence, reliability and compliance. The company that needs significant creativity has to engender deeper commitment that will justify the creatives putting more of themselves into their work. If the creatives know and share the values of the organisation, this is more likely to be a deal they welcome. If they are not energised by the company's aims and ethics, they'll look to go somewhere else with values more to their taste.

But even creative-friendly aspirational values, often crystallised by the founder of the organisation, can be diluted to homeopathic insipidity by successor CEOs addressing mergers and mission expansion; or, for those values languishing in my own academic world, simply left in Latin under our faux-medieval coats of arms.

Useful aspirational specialist values can also be formed lower down the organisation by key managers of creative colleagues. This is particularly helpful when the company's overall values have, perhaps because of the broad scope of the company's activities, become so amorphous that they provide insufficient handles for creative colleagues to grab hold of.

An objection to this argument linking institutional values to intrinsic motivation and high-level creativity, might be: 'But attractive institutional values are themselves surely extrinsic motivators and therefore damaging to creativity!' Well, no, because unlike general commercial motivators, good company values – being aspirational and therefore ultimately unobtainable – encourage the creative to stay in the creative maze longer, thus promoting rather than constraining creativity.

Finally, it might be wise for me to reiterate the metaphorical nature of Amabile's creative maze. I suddenly have a horrendous vision of an over-enthusiastic manager on a company away-day leading colleagues to a park's real maze and insisting they get inside – for a long time! – and down to some serious creating.

SUMMARY

- Most people usually do best at the things they enjoy doing most.

- For creatives, enjoying their creative process encourages them to come up with their best ideas. This is their intrinsic motivation.

- Extrinsic motivation doesn't help creatives do better work; indeed it tempts them to create at a lesser level by leaving the maze at the easiest exit that ensures they get the extrinsic reward on offer.

- A company with aspirational values attractive to creatives is more likely to win their support and therefore their commitment to stay in the maze longer and thus achieve high-level creativity.

- Aspirational specialist values can be formed and articulated by line-managers of creative colleagues as well as promoted more generally by directors in the boardroom.

FIBBER

"NO, IT'S NOT A LIE AT ALL, JUST THE WAY THINGS SHOULD BE."

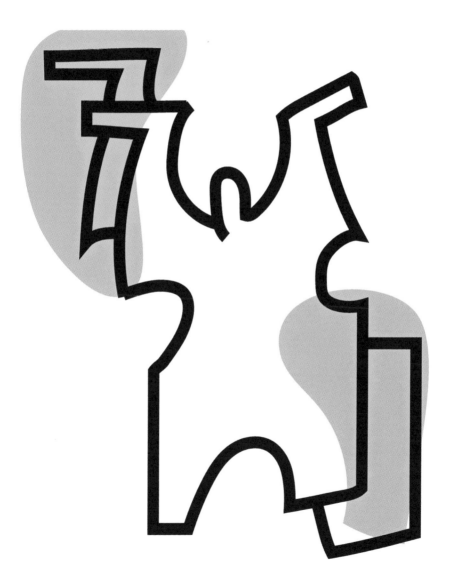

'Rules are meant to be broken'; it's a well known phrase. But is it a spur to greater creativity or a justification of antisocial behaviours? The answer that Francesca Gino came up with in 2014 for the Association for Psychological Science was that dishonesty and creativity might in some cases be two sides of the same coin.

'Fibber' is your colleague with a creative attitude to the truth.

You are in a planning meeting with her. She is in charge of an important element of the project, an element that must be completed before the next stage can start.

"Right Fibber…" you say, "So when do you reckon you'll get your bit finished?"

"No problem…" she replies, "Friday, by the end of the week."

You know that's not true. You know it can't be true; the job is too big. You know that Fibber knows it isn't true. You know Fibber knows you know it isn't true. So why on earth is Fibber claiming 'Friday, by the end of the week'?

Another chapter sketches Solo, the creative who isn't good in teams. He's a storyteller and Fibber is too, of rather tall-stories. But why does she have this compulsion? Perhaps her creativity depends on it?

On the surface Fibber's lies serve to keep you happy, for she knows that 'by the end of the week' is what you'd love to be true. And a little deeper than that, her lie keeps Fibber herself happy – it's what she too really wants to be true – for it would prove she's a great contributor to this important team project. And with that insight, the hint of storytelling starts to emerge linking her with Solo, her creative cousin.

Now, even deeper into Fibber's motivation: her ridiculously optimistic little story forms the goal for a big fantasy narrative, for if Fibber really worked amazingly hard, day and night, until Friday, she might actually succeed in completing her part of the project. So, her lie is an outline sketch for that nail-biting adventure story of our heroine, Fibber, who, despite the enormity of her task, struggles through to success, rescuing the project just in time, emerging with the product of her creativity, key to the project's success. In a sense therefore, Fibber's creative process is reliant on her storytelling that glimpses implausibly optimistic futures. They are lies, but probably necessary to Fibber's creative psychology.

But there are at least two other possible explanations as to why Fibber lies. The one that is probably the more useful for colleagues and managers of creative Fibbers is based on the observation that companies often celebrate creativity as a rare and special attribute of just a small subset of employees. This can create in those 'special few' a sense of entitlement, implying that the rules governing the behaviour of most colleagues do not apply to them; rules that include telling the truth. In the neat phrase of Vincent and Kouchaki in the *Harvard Business Review*, it is 'not just that creative people can think outside the box; it's that people who see themselves as creative, and see creativity as rare, believe they deserve a bigger box than others.'

I once reprimanded the director of a show for smoking during a rehearsal in the theatre. Clearly against the rules! He was furious with me. He was a creative: The Creative. The rule didn't apply to him!

From this 'entitlement' explanation of anti-social or dishonest behaviour flows a number of managerial actions you can take to short circuit that, arguably divisive, sense of entitlement.

Put simply: if an organisation wishes to mitigate creative lying by tackling a culture of entitlement it should decide that all colleagues are equally entitled, and therefore that none are. In practice, this will include promoting innovation wherever and whenever it emerges, through setting up structures that nurture creativity. These are summarised in Chapter 18 *Management models for creativity*. The result will be a normalisation of occasional creativity-related lying as a positive symptom of a creative organisation. Not to be ignored or celebrated, but openly and tolerantly challenged as a predicted fact of creative life: "O come off it, Fibber! You're never going to get your bit finished by Friday. When do you really think it'll be done by... the following Friday? What do you think rather than hope?" This approach allows Fibber to continue her subjective lying – crucial to her creativity – in a non-hostile and tolerant atmosphere, whilst allowing her organisation to schedule work on more realistic assumptions.

This response does however depend on the organisation recognising that all colleagues are at least potentially capable of creativity given a working environment that is conducive to innovation: a controversial opinion discussed in Chapter 2 *Are we all creative?*

In this egalitarian way, not only is Fibber a happier and probably more creative colleague, but creativity has been energised throughout the organisation. 'The Creatives' have been released from their claustrophobic, uniquely entitled silo and are now able to benefit from the enriching diversity of experience of their wider-ranging colleagues.

The third theory I can offer concerning Fibber's lies is, I confess, even more speculative and based on the fact that every significant creative project that Fibber – or indeed any creative – completes, changes her. She has, in a sense, superseded the Fibber of the past. Imagine her now looking back to that earlier edition of herself trailing all the opinions she once held, now frozen in her autobiography. As she gazes back, she sees there an erroneous understanding of today's Fibber. In a manner of speaking she is contemplating a lie.

People – by being creative – therefore inevitably turn themselves into liars. And there would be an unacceptable cost if they stopped lying; for without that constant invalidation of themselves, their creativity would also have to stop. Just as heat is energy, so creativity is change; and change, at least for Fibbers, is entangled with lying. Even if an attempt to moderate her fibbing were to succeed, most of her colleagues and managers would, I suspect, regret this attempt, for Fibber's identity and creative process is now undermined and thus her inventiveness compromised to the detriment of her own psychology and her company's innovative reputation.

I've suggested three reasons why creativity and lying may indeed be two sides of the same coin. The entitlement explanation opens the way to your being able to mitigate at least some of its divisive effects among your colleagues. My own 'it's because creatives are storytellers' theory may not, I fear, prompt so many management interventions, but might be useful to bear in mind when your entitled colleagues are telling you particularly 'creative' stories. My theory about creativity inevitably casting the creative – as focused through the partial lens of Fibber – as a recidivist liar should help you evaluate the degree of lying you're happy to tolerate in your company in exchange for her creativity.

CREATIVES, DEADLINES AND TEAMS

Creatives often find deadlines really annoying. Nasty things perhaps – but regrettably essential for most projects – and the creative must know his or her deadline and respond to it. I've never tried that old trick of telling creatives that the deadline is Friday when it's really the following Wednesday, in expectation that they will, as usual, not make the first date but probably manage the second. That subterfuge treats colleagues as children and thus makes more likely a childish response: "Well, I see through that, so I'm just going to take even longer!" A more effective tactic in my experience is to recognise that at the root of most creatives' dislike of deadlines is their admirable drive to achieve their best possible work. A deadline curtails that ambition. They therefore see themselves as victims of its imposition. Following an appreciation of the creative's disappointment, I've found that sharing the 'victimhood' with them is very helpful. So, when having to tell a creative that the old deadline has been brought forward by a week: "Yeah, I think it's really shit too, it makes things very tight and it's an absolute pain for all of us. Do you think there's any way you'll still be able to come up with something? Can I help at all?" is more likely to lead to a creative output from your colleague than: "Deadline's moved. Can't do anything about it… I'll need your bit a week earlier I'm afraid. No point complaining, just get on with it please!"

Gordon Torr suggests one interesting exception to the rule

that deadlines are unhelpful to creatives. He points out that exceptional work can be achieved when a group of colleagues is 'on a mission'. And this is true: I've seen it many times in the theatre when cast and crew work frantically in the days before a show's opening. A great sense of camaraderie emerges as the team pulls it out of the bag for the first night. Two interesting points, however, suggest that what I've been witnessing may not actually be creativity going on: first, the lengthy rehearsal process within the almost sacred space of the rehearsal studio is where the exploratory 'incubation' stage of creativity is undertaken, which then – still probably within the studio – morphs into directorial 'illumination' through working with and through the actors' own creative processes. The last-minute and wonderfully exciting 'we're on a mission' comes after this and is the pragmatic working out of the largely physical implications of the earlier creativity. What might, to the outsider, appear to be thrilling creativity is in fact mainly a sorting out of the mechanics of how the 'illumination' can actually work on stage.

The relationship between 'incubation' and 'illumination' on the one hand and the 'maze' (described in Chapter 8 *Why do I do what I do?*) on the other, is discussed in Chapter 14 *The creative process.*

The second revealing element of the 'we're on a mission' that points us away from celebrating a highly creative process, is that it's '*we're* on a mission' and we'll see many times throughout this book that creatives and teams can make uncomfortable bedfellows. Those fortunate enough to witness the excitement of the last few days before first-night will probably not be watching collaborative creativity, but instead the earlier creativity of the rehearsal now being voiced through the undisputed leadership of the director or stage manager as they attempt to get the team to deploy their craft skills in order to operationalise the earlier creative illumination now in danger of fading under the sheer physical difficulty of translating vision into reality.

Hard-line creativity scholars – those who are convinced creativity is a special and rare attribute, not on the same spectrum as its unimaginative cousin, problem-solving – come down very clearly against teamwork as an aid to creativity. Bonnie Siegler memorably proclaimed in her book *Dear Client* that 'vision is not a group activity'. I'm not convinced; but let's for a moment assume she's right, for it's a helpful idea with which to pick apart some key aspects of creativity.

As we'll see in Chapter 12 *Courageous companies: creative chaos*, creativity is unpredictable; indeterminate. Therefore, an environment that incubates creativity should promote indeterminacy. Does team working do this? Well, sometimes 'yes'. The unfettered tossing about of random ideas in a relaxed atmosphere where nothing is obliged to make sense or be practical, buildable or affordable and in which nobody feels foolish at coming up with the most outrageous idea – or indeed feels foolish at coming up with the least outrageous idea – is a creatively indeterminate environment. Yes, a creative team such as this is enriched by its free-wheeling and unpredictable style. But then, one of the team says…

"Right, so what we're saying is..." and a sensible, grown-up evaluative summary looms; then someone adds: "So what we need to focus on is…" and by implication most peoples' free-flowing ideas are in the bin. "Wow, that'd be expensive…" and it's goodbye creativity; hello pragmatism! "So what's our front-runner so far…?" Yes, high-spectrum creativity is definitely over for the day.

The person who came up with the 'front-runner' idea feels great, but the others are a bit deflated and the motivation for creativity becomes 'Who gets to be front-runner tomorrow?' or the prize of 'Yes, you're right, we could afford it that way': extrinsic motivations, destructive of the intrinsic joy of creativity and guaranteeing that the team will emerge from the creativity maze through an easy exit clutching a sensible, but mundane idea. That night at home when one of the team is asked if they have had a good day, it's: "Yeah okay, fine; you know…" If your company is content with creativity that is 'yeah okay, fine; you know…' then this kind of teamwork could be part of the answer. But if you need creativity that results in: "Sorry I'm late. I walked home the long way. I've got this amazing idea, so exciting… started at work this morning; maybe nothing will come of it, but maybe, just maybe…" If you need that level of creativity then conventional teams for significant creativity are probably not a good idea.

That's the case supporting Bonnie Siegler's assertion that 'vision is not a group activity'. But there is a plausible argument in favour of teams; even made up of creatives. The scene I painted saw a conversation that was very effectively prompting the emergence of creativity, descend into a bonfire of ideas. So perhaps the problem is not in teams themselves, but in their management.

Chapter 18 *Management models for creativity* notes the increasing incorporation of creative colleagues into project or account teams, which comprise a variety of skills such as marketing, manufacturing, design, scheduling and financial control. It suggests different management techniques for members whose job is principally the generation of ideas.

This is a useful idea here too; for the effective manager should not only be responsive to the needs of the creative members but also sensitive to the more pragmatic methods other colleagues must deploy. The first, and perhaps hardest, skill the manager of these mixed-mode teams needs to acquire is, therefore, the ability to recognise that team-working might be injurious to creativity. Mitigation relies on his or her understanding the nature and practice of creativity and its interaction with other ways of thinking.

If this understanding is achieved, the effective manager will let it inform the variety of mentoring styles needed and the choice of creatives to include on the team. Solo may, for example, be inappropriate, but Picky rather useful in a slightly annoying way. The timing of creatives joining and leaving a project should also be considered; as new ideas inevitably crystallise into timelines and budgets, a creative might withdraw, perhaps to bring his or her unusual vision to bare on a knotty sub-problem of the larger project.

So, do real teams actually exist? From this description of how the wise manager will customise his or her styles of leadership depending on the focus and motivation of each team member, it sounds more like managing a bunch of soloists than a single ensemble. And there is some truth in this; it would be a woefully ineffective manager who expected and demanded unanimity from his or her team. The bringing together – for the benefit of all – of a range of different talents obviously fuels a team's strength: defence, midfield, attack in a football team; or the even starker differentiation of a cricket team. If the manager really wants unanimity, he or she should quit the company and start running a rowing eight; although even there, there's a largely hidden variety of inputs. How about synchronised swimming? That might suit even better. Interesting that synchronised swimming has officially changed its name to 'artistic swimming'. Evidence, I wonder, that there exists – even beyond the dreamy bounds of creativity scholarship – a general disbelief in the abilities of undifferentiated teams to achieve anything much more than, well, an undifferentiated team; somehow disappointingly self-serving. I doubt the climate is right for a return of the Ziegfeld Follies, although it would brighten up Sunday night TV in the UK if the Tiller Girls were to fix their weirdly synchronised high kicking smiles once again. Musicians have a word for this: unison. Listen to more than half an hour of exquisite medieval unison liturgical chanting and you'll appreciate the diversity of harmony and multi-talented teams.

SUMMARY

- Deadlines – and especially changes to deadlines – should be supportively communicated to creatives. It is the job of the manager to translate the almost certainly deterministic tone of senior management's deadlines into a language and delivery that facilitates, rather than truncates, creative work.

- Managing a team that includes creatives requires the manager to deploy a sophisticated knowledge of the creative process in allocating tasks – and stages of tasks – to colleagues.

- Without informed and skilled management, teams attempting to achieve significant creativity will often underperform because its leadership has allowed the indeterminacy of creativity to be replaced by premature pragmatism.

WOBBLY
"...AND THEN SOMETIMES I HAVE THESE AWFUL DREAMS."

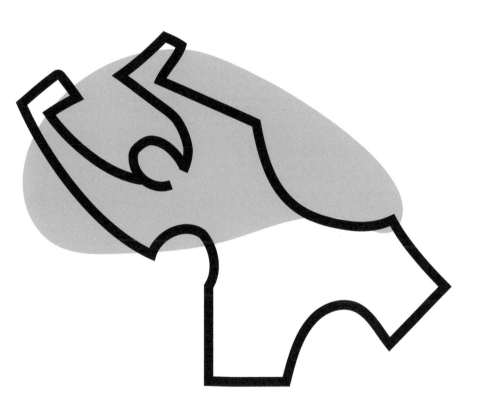

Why is Wobbly wobbly? Why are so many creative people wobbly? There are many reasons. Here are two: because they can't believe their luck will hold; and because every day they have to prove themselves from scratch. It might be helpful to ask yourself what your state of balanced composure would be like if you too doubted that you'd still have a job tomorrow or knew that your professional reputation was always being judged. A bit wobbly? This is the everyday world of Wobbly, for he creates things: new ideas; new products; new services; new procedures; new beauty; new anything. He relishes the process and gets paid for doing what he loves! 'Surely this can't go on; how can I stay so lucky? What if my luck changes; what will I do? I need my job!'

So, he can't believe his luck and that's because he doesn't think 'management' has the ability accurately to recognise his creativity. So how can he be confident in holding onto his job if those with the power to decide his future don't have the vision to appreciate his work and its value to the company? And perhaps Wobbly, in his darkest moments, shares management's supposed negative views of his creativity. Perhaps he finds it hard to believe that the creativity that has energised – even justified – his life thus far could evaporate and leave him with… well, who knows? He doubts his worth and thus his position; the job he loves is threatened. But you will have noticed that this was partly tied up with his negative view of 'management' and it's that issue that leads to the second reason for his wobbliness, the one about having to start from scratch every morning; what is the reason for this?

Creative employees often mistrust 'management': 'the suits', as they sometimes call them. Managers are seen as commercially focused and insensitive to the innovative skills of their creatives. This view is so ingrained that a creative colleague being congratulated by 'management' is sometimes seen by other creatives as having 'sold out' to the enemy; a very wobbling prospect indeed, for Wobbly's sense of professional self-confidence relies far more on the respect of his creative colleagues than it does on 'management' opinions.

So, Wobbly wants job reassurance from 'management' – but doesn't really value it even if he gets it – whilst at the same time desperately wanting professional reassurance from fellow creatives, some of whom are likely to be competitors; hardly a disinterested audience. It is not surprising that Wobbly doesn't bother to put his employee of the month certificate up on the wall of his office, but certainly does display the photograph of his getting an award at last year's Creatives' Dinner.

But even this sporadic applause from his creative peers isn't enough to settle his wobbles; he still feels that he has to start from scratch every day. And this is because both he and his creative colleagues know that they're only as good as their last piece of creative work. Their reputations are always provisional, subject to continuous reassessment – a wobble-inducing prospect – and because Wobbly lives for his creativity, assessments threaten a constant attack on his identity and sense of self-worth. Wobbly surely has every reason to wobble.

The *Minnesota Multiphasic Personality Inventory* is sometimes used by medical professionals when mental health problems are suspected. It accumulates a score for each client. The higher the score the more likely a mental health issue. Over the many years of its use, a pattern that correlates higher scores to occupations that traditionally call for significant creativity has been noted; so poets score highly and politicians don't. Wobbly will probably be near the top.

Most of the other creative caricatures in this book describe personality traits tricky for colleagues and managers to work with, but which are necessary if creativity is to be achieved. This has led to my suggesting that a successful attempt by manager or colleague at mitigating such a trait runs the risk of militating against his or her creativity; not a wise course of action for a company employing the creative for creativity rather than bland normality. But is this the case for Wobbly? Is his creativity dependent on his wobbliness? If he were – with a wondrous wand's wave – suddenly to become confident in the quality and ongoing longevity of his work, would his creativity be impeded, or perhaps boosted?

I think his wobbles are impediments to his creativity; mitigate these and an even more creative colleague will emerge. But there is one obvious objection to this assertion. Perhaps his nervousness about keeping his job – 'Can my luck hold?' – and his worries about the evaluation of his next piece of work actually spur him to greater effort and creativity, so his wobbles are valuable after all? No: this is not the way profound creativity emerges. Chapter 8 *Why do I do what I do?* discusses motivation and demotivation for creativity and concludes that extrinsic motivation impedes innovation. 'Keeping my job' and 'positive evaluation' are undoubtedly extrinsic motivators, urging Wobbly to end his creative searching at a superficial level; just enough to keep his job and get a little respect.

If your colleague's wobbles are solely or predominantly rooted in these or other extrinsic motivations, then lessening their impact can only assist Wobbly in achieving heightened levels of creativity. This conclusion of mine is supported by Amabile's view that the 'best atmospheres [for creative realisation of creative potential] appear to be those with little extrinsic constraint, little interference with work, and little cause for concern with problems (such as unemployment) that are extrinsic to the… problem itself.'

A brief complicating note, I'm afraid, about 'composite creatives'. You may recall from the introduction to this book that I underlined that neither Wobbly, Artiste, Molotov, Monk nor any of the other caricatures actually exist, being merely one-dimensional sets of abstracted characteristics. This being the case, your real life, multi-dimensional colleague may well demonstrate Wobbly's nervousness from time to time whilst simultaneously being a Solo who likes to work alone. You, Solo-Wobbly's manager, should decide to leave his solo preference untouched as, in all likelihood, a necessary precondition for his creativity; but attempt to mitigate his wobbliness.

Do you, as a manager, have a duty of care to those whom you manage? Legally speaking the answer will vary over different jurisdictions, but morally I hope the answer is simply: yes, of course. So, having decided to try and mitigate Wobbly's worries you should, of course, make sure he knows of the normal care, support and medical arrangements available to all employees. Facilitating professional help is superior to untrained and dangerous dabbling yourself. But what is within a manager's scope and power? Looking specifically at the two main worries with which Wobbly presented – 'Can my luck hold?' and 'What if my next piece of work isn't any good?' – you can make sure his creative achievements are publicly and loudly celebrated, with other creatives making most of the noise; if it comes just from you, the suit, it won't be so powerful and may just add to the pressure. You can also look at his contractual arrangements so that his length of guaranteed employment is as long as possible. You might also ensure he works on projects or accounts with supportive rather than competitive colleagues and consider how evaluation of his work is best delivered, perhaps asking Wobbly to negotiate its frequency with you, rather than simply imposing your own managerial timetable.

Wobbly is a valuable creative colleague. Indirectly reassuring him that he has less to worry about – at least at work – than he might imagine, can only make him yet more valuable and, incidentally, a more relaxed and easier colleague, too.

COURAGEOUS COMPANIES:
CREATIVE CHAOS

If your company relies, at least in part, on the creativity of its employees but senses its quality needs to be raised, you might look at what kind of environment regularly produces top-notch creativity and then replicate its key characteristics in your company.

Berlin in the 1930s. A city in which the established bourgeois order was being challenged by fascist popularism, tottering financial institutions, metastatic unemployment, a subversive counterculture and a moribund constitution. Here, Walter Gropius reinvigorated European design at the Bauhaus whilst Bertolt Brecht weaponised theatre, Ernst and Kokoschka envisioned new realities, and Kurt Weill created Mac the Knife.

Paris a decade earlier: Nijinsky, Stravinsky, Gertrude Stein, Picasso, Miró, Josephine Baker, Dali and Coco Chanel; all to the backdrop of desperate immigration – Coco C. is the only French-born creative on this list – and spasmodic reactions to revolutions abroad and political realignments at home following the cataclysm of the first world war.

Discomforting though it may be for the board members of today's creativity-light company, it seems cities in uncertain transition with competing ideologies, diverse populations selling different skills and speaking of alien cultures in strange languages, are just the places for great creativity. The board will need to have a steady nerve if it is to follow the model of Berlin or Paris, or Warhol's New York, or punk London, or renaissance Florence, or Periclean Athens, or Golden Age Baghdad; but the price of creativity is the chaos of diversity.

Is your company prepared to replicate these conditions for the sake of creativity? Well, some reassuring news: you probably just have to do so in certain limited areas of the organisation; and the new policy document that steers the development could be called something comforting like *Facilitating Creativity* rather than the frankly scary *Encouraging Company Chaos*. I suspect your board might be happier with that.

Let me guess some areas your existing policy documents address: recruitment; induction; appraisal; promotion; remuneration; complaints; whistle-blowing; corporate responsibility; and green issues? Even if you do call the new one *Facilitating Creativity*, will it sit comfortably with the others? You know better than I do because you've, of course, read them all from cover to cover, but my guess is *Facilitating Creativity* is going to stick out; for many of your existing documents seek to normalise behaviours, whilst your new creativity initiative releases colleagues from normality. It doesn't fit because creatives – particularly significant creatives – don't conform to ordered, defined, coherent, predictable patterns of work, just as those orgasmically creative cities, Berlin and Paris, didn't follow predictable and comfortable paths to their achievements. But your business needs the creativity of its colleagues, so an environment must be devised in which the 'chaos of diversity' can thrive within an otherwise ordered and commercially respectable company.

No two organisations will invent the same method of accommodating chaos within the order. But a common goal will be managerial processes still respectful of the ordered life of the company but which permit and encourage the chaos of diversity. If successful, the two hemispheres of this single world will be organisationally linked but ideologically very different.

Effective linking will often rely on comparatively junior managers of creatives skilled at translating and communicating the organisation's conventional apparatus of budgets and deadlines into the apparent chaos of a profoundly creative environment. In doing so, the mangers protect the intrinsically delightful playroom of creativity from the comparatively extrinsic work of the organisation, whilst simultaneously ensuring head office can keep polishing its targets. The link ensures that the targets are pursued by creative colleagues, albeit in an environment probably alien to that of head office.

The line-manager of creative colleagues, therefore, needs eyes in the back, as well as the front, of his or her head, gazing appreciatively towards senior management's goals and its necessarily ordered environment, whilst at the same time understanding and facilitating the unconventional world of his or her creative colleagues. The manager understands and speaks both languages, translating sensitively between the two. He or she is a key and cunning link, able to reassure both sides that their worlds are entirely legitimate and that neither has to worry too much about those weird people over there.

The manager's translations from company-speak to creative-language will probably include: the definition and presentation of project briefs; the communication of budgets and deadlines; the setting up of project teams; evaluation of creatives' performance; and recruitment of new creatives to enrich the multifaceted diversity of the creative pool. Translation in the other direction will often focus on procuring resources (space, personnel, budgets, time…) and gaining acceptance for unconventional modes of attendance, places of work, and unusual interactions with colleagues within and beyond the company.

But this might sound like I'm promoting apartheid: the establishment of an elite, a company within the company with its own permissive rules, customs, management and free-wheeling atmosphere. If so, I would also be tacitly accepting that the broad spectrum of creativity for which I argued in Chapter 2 *Are we all creative?* and which stretched from the most basic problem-solving – with the suboptimal table leg – to the heights of the Sistine Chapel's famous ceiling, is broken. It seems instead that I'm now supporting the opposite idea: that creativity is a rare attribute of precious few people who must work in an equally rare and precious environment. I do not hold this view. I'm still in the one-spectrum-wobbly-table-to-Sistine-Chapel camp. And, despite appearances, this continuous spectrum model of creativity is indeed consonant with the unusual creative environment I've outlined. I'll explain…

I'm simply urging good sensitive management that understands the environment necessary for deepened creativity and is able, pragmatically, to match this with particular projects that require protection from head office's extrinsically-geared method so inimical to truly innovative thought. If the current project is simple – a simple problem with a simple solution – then fine, not much shielding is needed at this end of the creativity spectrum. However, the next project could require innovation that cannot be built upon existing knowledge and that demands imaginative, uncertain and unpredictable ideas. This significantly creative project, with its undefinable process and unknowable outcomes, must not be staffed by colleagues forever worrying about timescales, budgets, holiday quotas and what to wear to the company picnic. This group needs shielding if it is to emerge from exit five of the creativity maze, excitedly gushing about a brilliant new idea.

A company today that is successful at drawing creativity from its employees will have comparatively junior managers as colleagues of creatives, not necessarily significantly creative themselves, but skilled at facilitating the creativity of others. The company will also possess, at its highest level, leaders who understand their need for creativity, are responsive to the demands of creativity and have the nerve to put in place the startling strategies that link the two. The next chapter *Facilitator* gives further details of a manager's challenging, but vital, role.

SUMMARY

- A company successful in nurturing significant creativity will encourage the development and continual refreshment of an environment that insists upon a diverse workforce of contrasting skills and aspirations.

- A manager, successful at facilitating creativity in such a tumultuous environment, translates both ways, between the ordered company and the disordered creatives.

The manager will be encouraged and trusted by senior management to:

- define and work within values supportive of creativity

- identify projects that require an exceptional working environment

- insist, when appropriate, upon an apparently chaotic environment

- work for ever-deepened diversity.

Additionally, the successful manager will have earned respect from the creatives which:

- allows him or her to criticise as well as champion their work

- encourages creatives to exit the maze at its higher levels

- awards the creative the right and duty to risk failure as a component of success

…whilst accepting that his or her own creativity is principally found within facilitating the creativity of others.

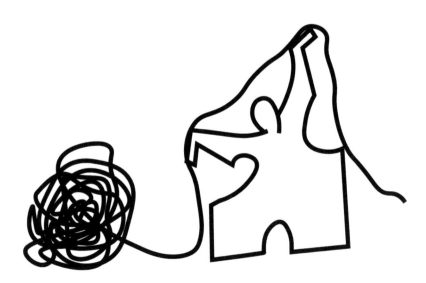

FACILITATOR

"YEAH, I KNOW... BUT THAT DOESN'T BOTHER ME BECAUSE IT'S NOT ABOUT WHO CREATES IT, BUT WHETHER IT'S ANY GOOD."

Chapter 12 *Courageous companies: creative chaos*, proposed
that companies anxious to release the creativity of their
employees should replicate – in a controlled way – some of the
characteristics seen in cities famous for their creativity. It noted
significant chaos and bewildering diversity in their populations.
The current chapter adds patronage to that list, and Facilitator is
today's company-based patron.

In Renaissance Florence, the wealth and artistic taste of the
Medici family allowed it directly to commission the finest artists
and their finest art. In 1920s Paris, the genius – and again,
refined taste – of Serge Diaghilev was able to bring together
diverse creatives such as Picasso, Stravinsky and Nijinsky.
Diaghilev had nowhere near the wealth of the Florentine Medicis
but did possess the commercial acumen to keep his Ballet Russes
company solvent; just.

Similar – in a way – was Andy Warhol's influence on cultural New
York in the 1960s. Through the respect he had gained for his own
creativity, Warhol was able, with his Factory, to encourage the
work of a generation of younger artists.

All three – Medici, Diaghilev and Warhol – were patrons:
respected figures of taste with sufficient resources to commission
new projects whilst retaining the sceptical and critical eye of the
connoisseur, intolerant of poor-quality work. 'Respected', 'with
sufficient resources', 'a critical eye', 'intolerant of poor-quality
work': ingredients, too, for the effective manager of creative

colleagues and for the hero of this chapter, Facilitator.

Pope Julius the second is quite famous, but not as famous as Michelangelo. Count Keyserling is also modestly well known by those fascinated by the geopolitics of eighteenth-century northern Europe, but I'll hazard not as famous as Johann Sebastian Bach. Patrons and the patronised. Such a pity 'patronised' has such a negative feel today; it's really not fair. Facilitator patronises her creative colleagues very helpfully indeed.

But does Facilitator really belong in my troupe of creative colleagues at all? Most of us have, after all, relegated Pope Julius to a footnote reminding us that he facilitated Michelangelo's ceiling of the Sistine Chapel. Note that we understand it as Michelangelo's and not Julius' ceiling. And it is undoubtedly Bach's Goldberg Variations, not Count Keyserling's: he just paid for them. Goldberg was, by the way, the Count's harpsichordist who played him the variations when he couldn't sleep. You can find some more 'facts' about him – woefully speculative I'm afraid – in Chapter 26 *Goodnight*.

So, following these models, our Facilitator seems doomed to uncreative obscurity in the company in which she works today, managing her creative – limelight hogging – colleagues. But before we forget her, let's at least consider what fellow contemporary facilitators actually do and measure their creativity in my steam-powered patent Creativity Spectrum Meter (CSM).

I choose me, and the project I facilitated in setting up Working With Creatives (WWC).

- I came up with the idea of forming WWC.

- Mine was the idea of using caricatures of commonly seen creatives as an approachable way into a complex subject.

- Then I recognised a need for a WWC website.

All, so far, clearly creative I'd immodestly claim. Its score on the CSM? Middle-ish.

Then I facilitated the creation of the WWC website, a task requiring some further creativity.

- Choosing a web designer with whom I could communicate and who seemed creative.

- Giving him a clear brief with defined objectives but no 'how-to-do-it' content.

- Being interested in his work and providing resources, but basically letting him just get on with it.

- Patiently tolerating all the missed deadlines.

- Praising his creativity.

- Evaluating, applauding and approving his work.

- Telling him to put his own logo on the website; his, not mine.

Clearly, this stage was largely spent facilitating the work of a creative colleague in much the same way as many frontline managers of creatives in any industry are likely to proceed, if allowed by organisational constraints. But creativity – perhaps scoring a 'low-medium' on the CSM – can still be seen. I devised the website's brief, had the vision to stand back from defining the website's 'feel', and had the creative nerve to accept missed deadlines as serving a greater good.

Finally, I did have some solid bits of my own creativity to slot into the completed website: descriptive text; video scripts; caricature definitions…

So, my work as Facilitator blended lower-spectrum creativity in facilitating the work of a colleague, with bits of more significant creativity. So I can confidently assert that my adoption of the name Facilitator indeed reflects the work of a creative manager. And the point here is that my facilitation will be recognised as familiar by our fictional caricature, Facilitator, in this chapter. So, finally we have an answer to 'Is Facilitator really a creative herself?' Yes, she clearly deserves her place in my posse of creatives.

Facilitator needs to be a connoisseur, a protector and a fan of creativity. Connoisseurs of fine art or fine wine don't need to know how wine is made or how to hold a paintbrush, but they must know how to recognise quality. Facilitator is in the same position. She doesn't – and mustn't – always come up with the creative ideas, but she must recognise and insist upon creative work of an appropriate quality.

As a fan of her creatives' work, Facilitator is its loud chief supporter. In this role she will argue for its importance in achieving company aims and thereby justify the ongoing provision of resources such as personnel, time, money, space and equipment. Given the apparently chaotic nature of creativity, Facilitator may also have to press for less predictable assets; perhaps exemption from normal office requirements such as defined working hours, location of work and reporting lines.

Facilitator also has to be happy with guard duty. Creatives need protecting from the bureaucratic procedures of normal organisational life. Businesses, for perfectly sound commercial reasons, need to be secure and predictable and this is achieved by a plethora of explicit and implicit rules, regulations and procedures; everything from parking spaces and dress codes to line management diagrams and promotion criteria. All fine, all useful and all ensuring – for laudable reasons – security and predictability. But creativity isn't secure and predictable; it is insecure and unpredictable. The most fertile environment for activating creativity needs to be a constantly diverse, vibrant, ever-changing reservoir of competing ideas, ideologies and practices. A 'secure and predictable environment'? Certainly not! The protection that Facilitator offers to creatives shields them from the organisation's security and predictability, for these surely limit the quality of their work.

Football fans love their clubs but do not accept poor performance for long or expect to be signed up as players. And Facilitator should take a similarly critical view of the quality of her creatives' work, but never try to take over their personal creative domains. Facilitator's innovative motivation for doing the job should principally come from the creativity she deploys when facilitating others' creativity. Her own significant creativity will not usually be seen much beyond the process-focused planning, initiation, monitoring and evaluation stages of a project. Facilitator will not attempt to join her colleagues in the creative maze whilst they are incubating and glimpsing the illumination of their ideas.

So far, I have sketched a rather rosy picture of Facilitator's professional life: a creative herself, initiating creativity elsewhere, keeping a close, knowledgeable and sophisticated eye on it all, and dipping in and out of process-driven details when she sees fit. Who wouldn't want to be Facilitator?

Well, there are downsides to the job. We have already seen with Pope Julius and the Count that the job doesn't come with much fame attached. But it may attract a lot of blame. "The resources she gave me were nowhere near enough; and that deadline, ridiculous! Doesn't she understand anything about creativity?" Then there's the creatives' derisive label stuck to her jacket –

SUIT – dripping implications of resource-obsession, aesthetic insensitivity, lack of creativity, being over-paid, dictatorial and 'one of them'. On the up-side, all Facilitator can hope for is some status and money from her managerial position; but these are extrinsic motivators, so will do nothing for her own creativity while further damaging her reputation among the creatives she manages. I suppose Facilitator might get to do the big speech at the product launch but will have to say that all the brilliance is down to the work of others, whilst silently hoping that her audience won't quite believe it. No, there aren't really many upsides to being Facilitator, unless that is, she truly appreciates the generosity and value of her creativity now directed to the achievements of others.

SUMMARY

From this analysis, Facilitator's job description will be daunting. How can her managers prepare her adequately to undertake the role? Training programmes will, of course, vary according to company needs, but many will seek to equip Facilitator with skills and knowledge allowing her to:

- understand the circumstances within which creativity flourishes and withers

- build and maintain a positive creative environment

- acquire the critical knowledge and taste to appreciate the quality of creatives' work

- translate company goals into creative motivation

- evaluate and explain the importance of the creatives' work to senior management

- protect her creatives from extrinsic worries about resources, budgets, deadlines, space, personnel etc.

- appreciate that much of her job satisfaction comes through the facilitation of others' creativity

- accept that her own opportunities for significant creativity might be rare

- expect senior management to recognise and applaud the huge value her creativity brings to the organisation

- require Head Office to award her sufficient autonomy so that she can become the Pope Julius II: the patron of her creatives.

THE CREATIVE PROCESS

Creativity is a process not an event. Hardly a eureka insight, but it does prompt an intriguing question: if it's a process, how does the process proceed? The answer to that question can guide managers and colleagues on the best – and worst – ways of working with creatives: the goal of this chapter.

To exemplify the creative process, I'll use 'the object' reproduced on the next page.

May I suggest that you spend several minutes with the object perhaps deciding what it actually is and what its message might be? Whilst doing so it would be helpful if you also casually monitored your emotions as you scrutinise it. Perhaps at times you'll sense delight, frustration, anger, excitement? At which stages of your scrutiny do these or other reactions hold you? Have a relaxed, frivolous wander around the object, but remain alert to things popping out: alert – as I'm sure you have guessed – to the process of your own creativity.

Although providing an adequate overall impression of the object, which in its original state measures approximately 73 by 53 centimetres, its reproduction here is too small to allow you easily to read its words. I'll therefore transcribe some of the text for you, not in any particular order, and not chosen with any goal in mind, but as you might encounter it randomly scanning the object at full-scale.

14

ANALYSIS OF THE CONTENT OF
RELIQUUM BY DISTILLATION AND HPLC

Isabelle Desjeux, Molecular Institute of Technology, Singapore, SG

Abstract
In this study, we undertake to analyse the chemical content of *Reliquum** with the goal of understanding whether their composition could explain the resilience of the species. We find that indeed, it can be distilled and subjected to HPLC. The result is surprising in that we find that *Profectus* is highly dependent on the survival of *Reliquum*.

Introduction

The study of *Reliquum* and its abundance in the labs led us to hypothesize that there must be a fitness benefit to the species for it to still be present despite all the setbacks, frustrations and other feelings it creates. With this in mind, we first checked the possibility of distilling the essential ingredient contained in *Reliquum* in order to analyze it further

Results

- *Reliquum* from different phyla contain carbohydrates that can be distilled (Fig. 1).

- An initial, informal analysis of *Reliquum* distillate on mice in the lab led us to suspect that the result of the distillation may create euphoria as well as bewilderment (Fig. 2).

- Further analysis by HPLC confirm that the distillate is indeed *Profectus* (Fig. 3).

- *Profectus* is a highly volatile and toxic compound (Fig. 4).

Material and Method

We have used only the purest form of Reliquum for this study, growing most of it ourselves for the purpose of this study, according to published method (See Desjeux, 2010). Each experimental round used between 500 and 800 kg of material. Distillation was done according to my grandfather's technique and the HPLC followed the instruction manual that came with the machine as well as colleagues' advice that would be too long to reproduce here.

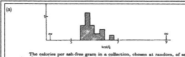

Figure 1 *Reliquum* contains carbohydrates that can be distilled (a) Carbohydrate content form different phyla (b) upon burning, *Reliquum* produces black remains, indicative of carbon-content (c) a lithmus test confirms the acidity of *Reliquum*, allowing for fermentation prior to distillation.

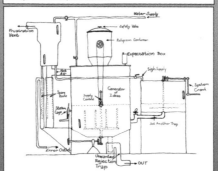

Figure 2 Mouse testing the intoxicating properties of Reliquum distillate

Figure 4 This picture was taken after Profectus exploded in our laboratory.

Figure 5 The distillation set required over 500kg of *Reliquum* to produce a few drops of distillate. Our distillation set-up closely resembled this one with the exception that the condenser was replaced by a cucumber, used for its cooling properties.

Conclusion

Profectus is present in *Reliquum*, in infinitesimal quantities.

Because *Profectus* presents such high toxicity levels, it is unlikely to be found at higher levels in *Reliquum*.

However, we humans are dependent on Profectus for our well-being. It is therefore essential to preserve the ecological balance by protecting Reliquum in order to prevent the extinction of Profectus.

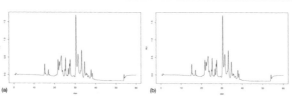

Figure 3 Comparing the profile of HPLC in *Reliquum* distillate (a) and in *Profectus* (b). The profile of Reliquum distillate HPLC was entered in the HPLC profile database; the profile for *Profectus* provided a 100% profile match.

* Reliquum: leftovers, failures, setbacks, rejections as they occur in the process of making science.
* Profectus: success, happy moments, forward steps, as they occur in the process of making science.

There are big letters at the top: 'ANALYSIS OF THE CONTENT OF *RELIQUUM* BY DISTILLATION AND HPLC'. Then, under that: 'Isabelle Desjeux, Molecular Institute of Technology, Singapore, SG.'

A large box is in the middle of the object. In it are arrows, each with a word or short phrase pointing to an element of its contents: 'Expectation Box'; 'Safety valve'; 'Frustration Vent'; 'Generator of Ideas'; 'Unwanted Rejection Trap'; 'Error Outlet'; 'Sigh Supply'… At the bottom of the box is some text: 'Figure 5 The distillation set required over 500kg of *Reliquum* to produce a few drops of distillate. Our distillation set-up closely resembled this one with the exception that the condenser was replaced by a cucumber, used for its cooling properties.'

The image to the right of the box looks like a mouse by the side of a glass jug. There is writing underneath: 'Figure 2 Mouse testing the intoxicating properties of Reliquum distillate'.

In the object's top lefthand corner a small box is headed 'Introduction'. Its text includes: 'The study of *Reliquum* and its abundance in the labs led us to hypothesize that there must be a fitness benefit to the species for it to still be present despite all the setbacks, frustrations and other feelings it creates.'

To the right of this 'Introduction' is an image of a gloved hand holding something with three distinct colours. Under this a text that includes, 'Figure 1 *Reliquum* contains carbohydrates that can be distilled...'

Above is an irregularly shaped, shaded element within a right-angled pair of lines. The text underneath starts, 'The calories per ash-free gram…'

Two boxes at the bottom left of the object display identical irregular lines. Below this is written: 'Figure 3 Comparing the profile of HPLC in *Reliquum* distillate (a) and in *Profectus* (b)…'

An image above shows a blank space under which appears, 'Figure 4 This picture was taken after Profectus exploded in our laboratory.'

Under 'Results' - centre left - two bullet points read, 'An initial informal analysis of *Reliquum* distillate on mice in the lab led us to suspect that the result of the distillation may create euphoria as well as bewilderment...' and 'Further analysis by HPLC confirm that the distillate is indeed *Profectus* (Fig. 3).'

In very small print at the right bottom of the object we are told, 'No animal was harmed in the making of this research' whilst in normal sized print headed 'Conclusion': '*Profectus* is present in *Reliquum*, in infinitesimal quantities. Because *Profectus* presents such high toxicity levels, it is unlikely to be found at higher levels in *Reliquum*.' Then, in large bold type: 'However we humans are dependent on Profectus for our well-being. It is therefore essential to preserve the ecological balance by protecting Reliquum in order to prevent the extinction of Profectus.'

Right, there's more I could report to you from the object, but that's probably as much as most people would observe when first studying it.

All clear? You understand now what the object is, the message it's conveying? You are now feeling content; any initial questions happily resolved?

No? But I bet you've at least wondered if it's something to do with science - that big box in the middle might have reminded you of school chemistry lessons, or perhaps the multicoloured object held by the gloved hand brought litmus tests to mind? But then there are the jokes, there's even a bit of lab equipment labelled 'Just another trap'!

So you could be forgiven for still feeling a bit puzzled about what the object is, and perhaps even more unsure about its message - if there is one - to you its observer. How do you feel about all this: bored, frustrated, annoyed, misled, even cheated? So, do you give up?

Tempting, but no, instead you resort to the Abstract towards the object's top hoping for some summary sense. Disappointingly, its text simply goes on yet again about '*Reliquum**' and '*Profectus.*' But an asterisk! Did you spot the asterisk? What's that for? And, at the bottom left of the object there's the asterisk again with two sentences in very small print presented (illuminated?) in white against the object's background that has now faded to dark grey:

'*Reliquum: leftovers, failures, setbacks, rejections as they occur in the process of making science.

*Profectus: success, happy moments, forward steps, as they occur in the process of making science.'

The message of the object is that success is dependent on
failure and that failure must therefore be protected if success
is to remain a possibility. It communicates this message though
visual allegory displaying a preposterous and hilarious scientific
experiment that distils failure, *Reliquum*, to discover that it
contains within it tiny quantities of success, *Profectus*.

Generalising only slightly, the object asserts that a creative
discovery or invention will be preceded by extensive searching
and evaluating, inevitably involving many failures and setbacks.
The object can therefore be seen to suggest that the creative
process is highly likely to involve a prolonged incubation
– riddled with unanswered questions, dead-ends as well as
occasional steps forward – before illumination lights up
understanding.

The other question I suggested you consider was 'What is it?' You
may have noticed that I have so far always referred to it as 'the
object' so as not to influence your creative process in inventing
your answer. Now, off the fence, possibilities certainly include:
a satire on scientific conference posters; a joke; an artwork; or a
manifesto of creativity. My answer to the 'What is it?' question?
All the above. But I have an unfair advantage, for I know the
object's creator, Isabelle Desjeux, a graduate of both science and
fine art degrees.

But I offered you a third task: a suggestion that you monitor your
varying emotional reactions as you casually wandered around

the object gradually becoming saturated in its language, imagery and allegory. I confess that my own period of saturation in the object lasted a disconcertingly long time for someone apparently knowledgeable about creativity. The artwork – I was clear about that at least – hung, misunderstood, on my downstairs toilet wall for several years. I knew it was something to do with how creativity happens but had failed to learn what *Reliquum* and *Profectus* actually were; hence my frustration. Then I read the footnotes and my mood changed to elation for I had discovered the key to the picture's meaning. But my success had taken several years – yes, really – of repeated failed attempts before illumination finally shone out. How was it for you?

When using this poster in creativity seminars, most attendees report mystification followed by a few speculative 'maybe it's about…' suggestions, before the footnotes prompt an exhilarating, and often remarkably loud: "Right, got it!" Reported emotions include mild interest, frustration, disappointment and elation, but perhaps doing the exercise alone and via a book is less energising; you don't have the thrill of criticising colleagues' ideas.

So Desjeux is arguing that the process of successful creativity must involve a lengthy period in which many failures will occur. The process of my creating my understanding of the artwork followed that same pattern: protracted questioning leading to eventual illumination. I suspect yours was the same, but I hope a bit quicker.

Several creativity scholars have suggested that the process of creativity often goes through three stages: saturation, incubation and illumination. How might Desjeux's own creative and practical process completing her artwork articulate this abstract model? Being both a professional scientist and professional artist constituted, I suspect, a thoroughly saturating experience. Her planning and drafting of the artwork must surely have involved changes of mind, false moves, minor successes and yet more setbacks: her incubation phase, leading to illumination when she knew what she wanted to do and at least the outline of how to do it. So Desjeux's artwork is not only the product of her own use of this tripartite general theory of creativity, but is also an explanation of it for us, her audience. The process you went through to arrive at your illumination, this too was a creative process that probably followed a similar pattern. Your saturation occurred as you first became casually acquainted with the image, incubation as you suggested and tested various hypotheses about what the image was and what it might mean, and finally the illumination of: "Right, got it!"

I've suggested that Desjeux's saturation probably preceded the creation of this specific artwork which illustrates just the incubation and illumination stages. Desjeux's saturation came whilst immersing herself in the subjects of science and fine art. It was, in a manner of speaking, a general saturation not yet connected to this or any specific output, but a familiarisation with the way those subjects work, their vocabulary and grammar. She was learning the craft of her bi-polar subject, wandering around creative processes that would later incubate into a multi-polar illumination, and into creativity that plausibly links all particular examples of this human preoccupation.

Many scholars of creativity have noted that creativity is a practical activity. A person claiming to be 'creative' but who is unable to exert that creativity through a particular medium — music, art, accountancy, the law, design etc. – can, in common parlance, hardly claim to be creative at all. Creativity needs to be rooted in the practical reality of expertise in a craft (Chapter 22 *Creativity in your R&D department* expands on this idea). The saturating acquisition of craft skills is a step on the spectrum of creativity. It's an exploratory rather than experimental stage, sometimes one of apparently aimless wandering but which nevertheless rewards the wanderer – as long as he or she is alert and open to the possibility – with knowledge invaluable in the higher reaches of the creativity spectrum. Gosh, we're in deep waters here with polemical art and allegorical saturation, and we haven't yet considered 'the maze', that metaphor from Chapter 8 *Why do I do what I do?* How does it fit into the general theory of creativity we are now inspecting? Blissfully easily actually: it's just the alternative name for incubation and illumination.

You'll recall that 'the maze' is the imaginary place in which a creative incubates his or her ideas. It has five exits of increasing illumination. The job of the creative is to stay in the maze – energised by intrinsic motivation – until the illusive and demanding higher level exits are found. It's the job of the creative's perceptive manager to shield him or her from the extrinsic motivators of normal commercial life which tempt the creative towards the maze's easily found, but creatively barren exits.

But let's examine that maze/incubation assertion that the creative needs to spend a long time there if high-spectrum creativity is to emerge. Clearly, 'a long time' is to be understood as a metaphor rather than a stopwatch rule. A more accurate translation of 'a long time' is 'as long as is necessary for the creative to have considered and tested all possibilities to permit him or her confidently to assert that his or her idea to be brought to the world is the best his or her degree of creativity could devise'. More accurate, but perhaps we'll just stick with 'a long time'? Recall those two footnotes on Desjeux's art that were essential to our understanding of her message, but hidden. Why hide them? Perhaps because they result in our incubating in her maze longer, experiencing first-hand the creative process about which she is teaching us.

Imagine that Desjeux has now returned to her laboratory as a research scientist working, principally alone, on an innovative project, and you're her manager. You're lucky: she's certainly creative – with Playful's sense of fun and Molotov's divergent determination – but how should you foster that creativity and particularly her maze-based process of incubation and illumination? I suggest the following, not only for Desjeux but for many creatives...

- Understand and appreciate the process of creativity.

- Define her brief so the 'edges' – not the content – of eventual illumination are clear.

- Provide adequate resources and shielding from extrinsic motivation; especially deadlines.

- Celebrate failures and setbacks as indicators of success.

And then stand back and let the creative just get on with it.

MONK

"WELL, YOU'VE GOT TO BELIEVE IN SOMETHING."

Do you have a creative colleague whose quality of work fluctuates between mundane and superb? He sometimes works hard, but only on certain projects?

Perhaps you're his manager and noticed when you recruited him that he had moved from employer to employer rather more frequently than normal. Watching him around the office you see he's a bit of a loner and takes little part in any of the social activities which you've set up to promote teamwork. You have no idea how to motivate him. He's the creative hero of this chapter.

Monk's basic issue is that he doesn't actually believe he's working for the company that employs him; instead he considers, in a profound sense, that it's the company that's working for him. He feels it's his right to do the creative things he loves; so, for him, it's the duty of a company to employ him to do them. His subjective reality is more to do with the employer facilitating his ambition than the other way round. He doesn't so much have a job as a 'vocation' and that's why his name is 'Monk'. When he's seen in large organisations he will often appear discontent, perhaps dreaming of running his own business. If he achieves this goal, his unwavering laser devotion to his vocation often makes him difficult to work for. The happiest Monks are those who can express their calling through a hobby. But your Monk needs to earn a living and has the creative skills that could be extremely useful to the company.

I once had a particularly brave manager who sat me down one day and simply asked: "What motivates you at work, Alastair?" I'd never been asked that before and I'd never asked it of myself. I was shocked: it felt impertinent, almost as if I were under attack. I had no idea of the answer and blurted out some cliché about money and status. I've recounted this little story because I found it so surprising that I should be asked the question; and that's ridiculous, for my manager's question surely searched for the most valuable piece of information needed to build a happy and effective employee. This chapter discusses Monk's unusual motivation for work, a motivation that his manager needs to understand.

Colleagues differ and their motivations for work differ. The subject is complex and broad; and my only reason for opening this Pandora's jar is to show how different Monk's motivation is from those more commonly seen. Monk is suspicious but prepared to risk doing a deal with his company: "Give me freedom to do the job my way and I'll do what you want as long as you demonstrate that your aims fit my destiny: my vision of what I was born to do."

Much more popular with most employees not known for significant creativity is the compromise deal: "I'll work for you as long as the job is legal, fulfilling and pays enough for me to live most of my real-life outside work..."; but not far ahead of the pragmatic: "Money motivates me. The actual job I do is irrelevant, but I do like to live reasonably comfortably. So I come to work to earn enough money to buy that life." If most managers' experience comes from working with colleagues in the last two groups, they will indeed find Monk tricky to motivate.

Chapter 11 introduces Wobbly who can't believe his luck in still being paid to do what he loves doing. Monk is his opposite, seeing no reason to believe that he might not always be so fortunate. But perhaps Wobbly and Monk are in fact the same person: Wobbly on a bad day; Monk when feeling confident?

So far, I've made Monk sound arrogant and entitled, and that's really not fair, for he's a valuable creative colleague. It's true he's not going to bother with that email you sent about the new parking arrangements, but he is going to focus one hundred percent on his current company project as long as it also helps fulfil his own creative goals. So, when engaged on suitable pieces of work, he'll be happy and so will your company.

What's Monk like to work with? Most of the time absolutely fine. He's dedicated, determined and often produces excellent work alone or in like-minded teams; he doesn't get on with Playful though. It is true that Monk isn't likely to be your most flexible colleague, for he's single minded about his vocation and uncomfortable when prompted to challenge its borders. He can be blinkered at times, but as long as his tunnel vision is roughly in line with company needs, everybody's happy.

His dedication and commitment are unshakeable. But this

dedication and commitment are not actually in support of his employer; he is certainly not a 'company man'. I'll explain…

I'm a football fan. I support the English side, Tottenham Hotspur. I started when I was six and will support them until I die. Football fans don't change clubs, unlike the players who move around all the time. And we fans accept that; even understand it. We appreciate that players have a higher order of loyalty than we do. Their vocational loyalty is to football – and its rewards – rather than the particular club that currently employs them, whilst a fan's primary loyalty is to a club rather than football. I'm content to see Tottenham play rubbish football; as long as we win.

And Monk has that higher level of loyalty: a loyalty to his creative vocation way beyond the particular company in which it is currently practised. But you really don't want him to go to another team. He's one of your star players; so how can you stop him switching?

The answers are actually quite straight forward, but they do rely on your company recognising Monk in the first place, understanding his real motivation for coming to work, and then attempting to align that motivation with the direction of the company. The wise manager will quickly spot Monk from his somewhat unusual combination of inflexibility and dedication: on the one hand unhelpful – even destructive – but combined with excellent work that is likely to be on-time and within budget. His observant manager will recognise that all depends on whether Monk's heart is really in the current project.

From this point, the sensible manager will dig deeper into Monk's motivation. This could, of course, be done through the formal appraisal process, as long as this avoids the common charade that quickly morphs: "And what are you personally looking to achieve working here?" into: "What you have to achieve here is…" The goal is to try and locate Monk's vocation within the aims of the company for which he apparently works. From the identification of a ladder stretching from personal ambition to company aim, could emerge a content, productive and effective colleague.

I recognise that the value of erecting such a ladder is useful for all employees, not just Monk. But for him it is not simply useful, but vital. Most employees, when faced with tasks that don't really fit their personal aims, will simply shrug, moan a bit and get on with it. Monk won't: he'll quit. And Monk is good at his job when it suits him; you don't want him to go.

My work over many years with a wide range of creative colleagues suggests that one of their more attractive shared characteristics is a sympathy for what might be called high-minded and altruistic goals. In my experience, few creatives are searching for money, for they find creativity much more fulfilling. If I'm right in this, a course of action for getting Monk on-board with the company appears: make sure that the company's high-level Aims and Values are likely to be attractive to creative colleagues. A company whose success depends on the creativity of its staff is very likely to suffer a damagingly high turnover of key colleagues if its stated aim is, for example, simply to increase shareholder value. Monk is more likely to be able to locate his vocation within a more socially progressive and broadly defined aim, such as: 'Our goal is to promote health through developing medicines for the world.' And, of course, if successful, this company will simultaneously – but more quietly – increase shareholder value.

This may sound like a cynical ploy, a trick to ensnare the naive but valuable Monk. But it's not; for what sensible company would set up or perpetuate a working environment that dissuades talented creative applicants from joining, makes more likely the departure of those who have nervously joined, and undermines the work of those just about able to tolerate its culture?

Monk is unlikely to become an effective manager of creative colleagues. His determined servitude to his vocation makes it unlikely that he will possess the empathy needed to accommodate others' goals. As a manager he would, therefore, probably appear cold and unsympathetic. However, promotion is a distinct possibility. His creative work can be superb, so he will have been noticed by senior management impressed by his dedication in apparently working toward the goals of the company; surely characteristics that should be spread more widely through promoting Monk. The mistake being made is in reading Monk's alignment with company goals as dedication to the company, when in fact it simply indicates that Monk has generously decided that the company is good enough to be working for him.

Monk is creative, never likely to be a popular colleague, and tricky to manage, but an employing organisation that recognises that it is Monk who's employing them, and has the nerve to work within, rather than against, this unusual reversal of roles, will have a colleague who makes valuable creative contributions to well-crafted company aims.

CREATIVES AND EVALUATION

In Chinese culture, some mothers practice confinement for a month after giving birth. Traditionally, neither mother nor baby leaves home during this period. The reason apparently concerns Chinese medicine's view that both are particularly susceptible to illness during this period and must therefore avoid the outside world. Fine, that's reasonable. But the commonest interaction of a new-born with the world beyond the front door is, in my experience, carried out to evaluative choruses of: "How cute!"; "What lovely eyes!"; and "I'm sure he'll grow out of it…" I wonder if Chinese medicine's hesitation is based on a quiet understanding that evaluation that comes too soon can be just as hazardous as infection?

And evaluation has also to be faced by creatives at work and handled with similar care by their midwife-managers; for evaluation – or more precisely, a creative's desire for positive evaluation – is an extrinsic motivator tempting the creative to an early departure from the intrinsic rewards of the maze. In addition to this concern, the nature of creativity – investing not only in professional craft expertise but also personal vocation (Monk), identity (Artiste) and fears (Wobbly) – makes giving a creative evaluative feedback – even of the most supportive kind – an extremely sensitive undertaking. But it is an unavoidable task. To hide creatives from the facts of professional life would be patronising and infantilising.

One way in which personal collateral damage can be minimised is to follow Amabile's good advice and ensure, as far as possible, that feedback focuses on the work, not the person who is producing the work. So, even at the level of the vocabulary used by the manager: "What you have done is…" and "What you should do is…" might be consciously replaced by: "What this work does is…" and "The work should go on to…" Given the strength and depth of the relationship between the creative and that which he or she creates, I'm not certain that this approach will greatly ameliorate the inhibiting nature of evaluation, but it might serve to at least remind the deliverer of the evaluation to tread as lightly as possible.

I once went to a concert where a friend was performing a particularly difficult violin sonata. After the show, I went immediately to her dressing room to congratulate her on a fine performance. After assuring her – repeatedly – that her playing was great, I conceded that one passage in the last movement might just have been a tiny bit out of tune. She exploded: "Don't you know the 24 hour rule?" I didn't. "You must not say anything negative, nothing at all, absolutely nothing critical, until 24 hours after the performance! I'll be able to take it then, but not until!"

Why should this particular creative, and probably most creatives, be so touchy about even the mildest criticism? Because it came too early. The creative process of my friend was still winding down. She was still in her creative maze and there I was dragging her out of it with talk of a minutely out of tune G#. It was detrimental to her own reflection on her performance that was still incomplete.

Generalising now: you, the wise manager of creatives, should delay evaluation – and especially public evaluation and contribution to a creative's new idea – until he or she has completed its birth and is ready for the world to admire and question it. In a way, this suggestion relates back to Chinese medicine's advice about avoiding human infection, for I am proposing that a creative's manager should similarly protect the product of that creativity from 'infection' from outside.

If followed, this strategy should certainly dissuade you from arranging focus groups to comment on 'what ideas they've got so far; we can steer them in the right direction' and should even warn you away from too many corridor conversations that start with: "Had any good ideas yet?" You will be told when they have. To do otherwise, and insist on a running commentary on your colleague's inevitably stuttering process, will: to Artiste, appear that you're trying to kidnap her children; to Solo, that you're trying to highjack his project; to Monk, that you're questioning his commitment; to Playful, that you're accusing him of wasting time; Picky won't mind it; but Fibber will fear you're challenging his world view; whilst Molotov will regard your question as a gross management invasion of her rights as an autonomous human being. The only creative who will reply with: "Oh, thanks for asking. Actually, it's very interesting at the moment. Some ideas seem promising; others not so much. We could chat about it over coffee if you like? But first tell me how you're getting on managing us all: nightmare I should think?" And who is this? Facilitator of course. You've always 'clicked' with her, and that's because as a manager, you're probably a facilitator too.

One last example of wisely delayed evaluation. You might recall the fictional story of Chapter 8 *Why do I do what I do?* about you, the vacuum cleaner and the new metal alloy. After you had experienced your highly creative idea that it might be useful in jet engines you …

'… *don't yet chat to colleagues about it, but after a few days you go to see your manager and suggest she might want to have a preliminary look at possibilities* …'

You realised consciously or subconsciously that you were still emerging from the maze and that your idea, so newly born, was not yet strong enough for public comment or questions.

SUMMARY

- The manager and colleagues of creatives should be sensitive about the timing, frequency and rigour of evaluation. Too early, too often or too muscular and the creative will feel attacked and may respond with anger rather than appreciation that others' comments can be helpful.

SOLO

"I JUST NEED TO SEE THINGS THROUGH FROM START TO FINISH. WHAT'S WRONG WITH THAT?"

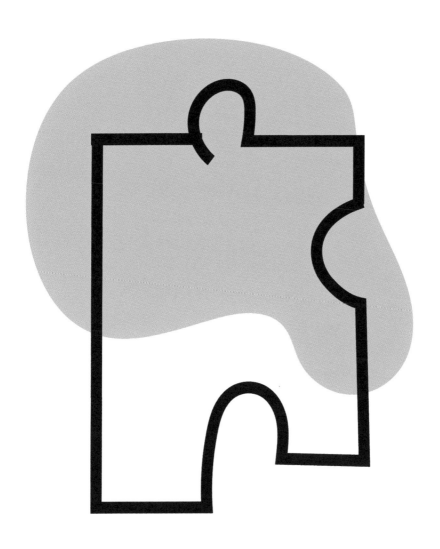

Does Solo work in your company? He's very creative but hopeless in teams.

If your company's success depends on the creativity of its employees, it makes sense to develop working practices that get the highest levels of creativity from those colleagues. And this can be tricky, for most creative people are not famous for getting up in the morning to contemplate how their personal creativity can be yet more closely aligned to the company strategic plan. Unless, I guess, they own the company.

How to get Solo doing his best creative work for you? Solo's great when left alone but most of your company's projects require a team of cooperating colleagues and Solo just clams up when he's forced to attend. The key thing is to recognise, then accept, that Solo is a soloist and to stop urging him to morph into an ace collaborator. He isn't going to manage it and his creativity, in fact, requires him to be solo. So, any managerial attempt to get him to change will undermine his ability to be creative; and that's why you hired him in the first place.

If asked about his problem with teams he might say: "My really good ideas, the ones that are genuinely new and exciting, just don't emerge when I'm in a team. No: teamwork seems to hold them back, sort of stifles them even as they're being born in my brain." And this observation probably has some truth in it for, when working alone, Solo is able to see an argument through from beginning to end, to develop its narrative and let its story unfold at its own pace. When coerced into a team, that narrative, still groping for its direction, must allow others to influence its course, content and goal. There are but few examples of really good novels written by more than one author. Alone, Solo relishes the responsibility of expressing his own creativity in his own way, accepting the risk of failure rather than the safety of dissolving anonymously into the corporate soup.

But the key point about Solo's preferred way of working is the quality of what he produces. When permitted to gestate his own creativity, he produces his best work: innovative, disruptive, original, authentic. Do these words characterise the outputs of many of your teams? Solo's process – if you can use that word to describe his apparently chaotic creativity – is probably based on saturation followed, in the maze, by incubation, ending in illumination, as outlined in Chapter 14 *The Creative Process*. He is professionally saturated in his specialist area of work, then he lets the particular project he is now working on incubate in his brain – perhaps forming novel links with other ideas, perhaps zooming off in unpredicted directions – before illumination occurs and a brilliant bit of creativity sometimes pops up, entirely unreliably. This saturation, incubation, illumination sequence may take minutes, weeks, or may never be successfully completed; but when it does, Solo's creative results can be spectacular.

How does this compare with an established model of team-working in which Saturation, Incubation, Illumination, is replaced by Forming, Storming, Norming, Performing? Here, doable outputs are the goal ushered in by timescales, budgets, agendas and sandwich lunches. This is, however, not to say that team working is bad and Solo's style is good; for, if your company has a problem that needs solving, it's wise to recruit a team of appropriately skilled experts onto it. Perhaps you're a manufacturer of cranes and your new Big Beast keeps tipping over. A team of technical experts will sort it out far more effectively than Solo. Stabilisers, suitable ground conditions, weight/reach calculations: don't invite Solo to join the team. "I wonder how we might build cranes for use in space – zero gravity – that's interesting…"

So, the conventional team is good at solving defined problems, but less successful at more open-ended creative thinking, and one reason for this is that conventional teams tend to seek consensus after the Storming phase has been fought through, and consensus is usually achieved by rooting decisions in existing ideas or practices; the comfortable status quo invigorated by a bit of inching evolution. Solo's saturation, incubation, illumination process avoids the quicksand of consensus by insisting on the primacy of his own meandering creative narrative.

If your company's current key project is to ensure next year's audit goes well, a team is best. If, on the other hand, it's to be an entirely new product, then Solo is a better bet. But the two can touch: if Solo comes up with a creative, zany idea for that new product, you'll then need a good pragmatic team to work out how it can be manufactured and how much it should cost.

And it's this sequence of competence that starts to solve the managerial problem of how best to exploit Solo's creative talent. Accept that his way of working will often defy conventional business practice with its teams, deadlines, budgets, and common sense, but recognise he has huge creative value as long as you just let him be Solo.

MANAGEMENT MODELS FOR CREATIVITY

Managing for creativity and managing for more widgets needs different strategies.

This chapter explains why the traditional industrial model of management doesn't work for creativity and why today's more enlightened alternatives must also be applied intelligently if the organisation is to deepen or widen its pool of creativity.

A fictional account of your creative interest in a new metal alloy appeared in Chapter 8 *Why do I do what I do?* to illustrate extrinsic and intrinsic motivations. Here, it is examined in order to evaluate management strategies.

Some questions and answers about your experience with the vacuum cleaner and its new alloy:

Q. At what point were you most creative?
A. At the moment of curiosity when the question of the alloy's possible relevance to jet engines came into my mind.

Q. How long did this creativity take?
A. A second?

Q. How was that creativity managed?
A. Managed? It wasn't managed at all!

Q.   Were you at work?
A.   No, at home.

Q.   Why were you working at home?
A.   It wasn't work.

Q.   Why did that vacuum cleaner curiosity come to you?
A.   Maybe my partner's comments; the random magazine; maybe a dream? I don't know. It just happened. Haven't a clue really...

Q.   Would you have got this vacuum cleaner curiosity at work?
A.   Probably not. There's a lot I really have to get on with there.

And indeed, you do have a lot to do in your paid job at work adjusting two troublesome components controlling the fuel to power ratio of a jet engine. But you are slipping behind schedule and starting to realise that the job will take longer than anticipated; the budget may well be exceeded. You discuss the problem with your manager. She reminds you, kindly, that it is a very important project, which, if successful, will help your company sell a lot more engines (note the extrinsic motivation she's using). Then she adds, a touch more urgently, that both your professional reputations – and bonuses – depend on its working (more extrinsic motivation).

Your manager, then, with some administrative difficulty, employs two additional engineers to work with you, sources more testing

equipment and introduces a second shift. It was hard for her
to organise, but she's good at her job and worked through
the admin, managing to get the new resources approved and
delivered quickly. She's happy; you're happy. The project is back
on schedule.

Perhaps a rather rosy view of the good old industrial model
of production? Yes certainly; but one suggesting that getting
appropriate resources – skilled personnel, time and equipment
– in place and in balance with acceptable costs, is helpful in
generating the planned results. It's also worth noting that the
manager's use of extrinsic motivation was fine; not damaging
in the least. She probably didn't need to lay it on quite so thick
but in this traditional manufacturing technique of managing, it
seldom does any harm; for employees are indeed motivated by
external incentives such as bonus payments. Your problem with
the jet engine was solved through good management suited to
the issue. Contrast this with the way your creatively insightful
moment with the new alloy was managed. "Managed? It wasn't
managed at all!"

Imagine now that you've left your very successful – although you
confess, rather repetitive – job, adjusting engine components, and,
as a result of the alloy incident and a few subsequent similarly
random insights, have become your company's first CIG (Creative
Ideas Generator). You got on really well with your boss before, so
you're happy that you're still reporting to her from your new role.
You're chatting:

"Right, welcome back. This is your work cubicle now, okay? Usual 9-5 working day… Oh, so you get your best ideas away from the office? Tricky. And they appear at any time? Tricky.

"Right, well anyway, I expect ten ideas a week, on my desk every Friday by 4.30 please… Oh, so some weeks there might not be any; some weeks loads? Tricky.

"Right, so I'll put more people into your team on lean weeks to smooth production flow. So when will those happen? We can schedule them for HR to action; that'll sort it… Oh, so you say you usually get your ideas alone and most will lead nowhere? Tricky.

"Right well, I'll just put in a few quality assurance experts; that should solve it… Oh, and you don't know where your ideas come from; sometimes you just dream them? Tricky.

"Right, no problem. I'll appoint a head of dream monitoring and set up a dormitory in your department… Oh, you want to go back to component testing? Look, don't do that. I hear you're in line for employee of the month and that comes with guaranteed car parking space for thirty days; it's right next to mine!"

The model of managing for industrial productivity is likely to be less than helpful when managing creatives. Or, quoting Davis and Scase, 'To manage and organise… creative colleagues it is necessary to apply different assumptions, methodologies and principles of organisational behaviour to those used when monitoring the tasks of factory workers…'

A reader of a book called *The Characters of Creativity* may be forgiven for assuming the issue is all about the creative people who are doing the work. The quotation from Davis and Scase is a useful corrective to this partial view, for it reminds us of the importance of 'organisational behaviour'. Indeed, Amabile's top ten 'Environmental stimulants to Creativity' and top ten 'Environmental obstacles to Creativity' all focus on the way an organisation behaves.

So, what are the ways in which creativity can be accommodated within an organisation needing its insights? Davis and Scase suggest four possibilities: Incorporation; Demarcation; Clustering; and Segregation.

- Incorporation: creatives retain their specialist role but are managed within conventional organisational structures.

- Demarcation: creatives are identified and managed differently from other employees.

- Clustering: creatives are employed by specialist creative companies that 'cluster' around – and are employed by – other companies which don't have those particular skills or facilities in-house.

- Segregation: creatives are self-employed and work alone – writers, composers, artists, inventors… Their income comes generally from advances, royalties, commissions and self-financing.

Of these four mechanisms, the most fashionable today for organisations of significant size and complexity is incorporation. Here, creative colleagues maintain their roles as initiators of innovative and useful ideas, but within an account or project team that has other concerns, too: budgets, deadlines, brainstorming, focus groups, marketing, sales projections…

The predicted advantage of incorporation is honourable: the creatives' work can now be informed by, and grounded in, the exigencies of 'real life' and their creativity enhanced by understanding more of the manufacturing, marketing and sales environments in which their creations must thrive. The creatives' manager might additionally claim they will find it helpful and interesting to be able to see the project through.

Under incorporation, the creatives still have their divergent ideas, but managing them is normalised, for the creatives are now in groups of complementary colleagues enjoying the company's conventional managerial levers of assistance and control. The problem of managing creatives is solved by making them comparatively normal, one of us.

If you have made it all the way to this point in my book, you will have spotted the flaws in this 'solution'. The creatives now have a number of new inputs into their creativity: sensitivity to budget; adherence to deadlines; responding to brainstorming comments and focus group outcomes; sympathy to marketing's views and sensitivity to sales projections. All extrinsic, all urging the creative to produce work that will satisfy those voices wanting them to leave the creativity maze at a 'good enough' level that is compatible with their own extrinsically-focused criteria of success.

So, the sensible company has realised that the industrial production model is hopeless for managing creatives and chooses the incorporation alternative, which indeed makes life easier for the firm's management structure diagram but undermines the creativity of colleagues. The neat solution is in fact just another problem but, nevertheless, increasingly popular.

We might be forgiven for wondering if some companies really want the creativity they champion so loudly in their away-days, team-building exercises and annual reports, for they seem remarkably adept at implementing new ways of crushing it. Perhaps subconsciously they consider creativity, and its attendant chaos and uncertainties, to be all a bit of a nuisance really?

Returning to the four options for obtaining creativity, the second, demarcation, is clearly highly attractive. By identifying and separating the creatives from the unhelpful extrinsic motivations of the broader company, the special management techniques outlined elsewhere in this book can be applied comparatively easily. Graham Torr puts it well: 'For creativity to flourish it is imperative to allow autonomy, nonconformity and indeterminacy. Without these, colleagues with intellectual capital will be reluctant to exploit their own personal creativity for the overall goal of their employing organisation.' And there is evidence that this demarcated approach works. The professional theatre has long considered its director, lighting designer, set designer, costume designer and sound designer, to form The Creative Team. But there is a downside to the demarcation solution: an elite, tiny cadre of privileged colleagues is established, excused from modes of behaviour demanded of others and damaging to the egalitarian 'we're all in this together' principles of many contemporary companies. Whilst watching a show one might wonder at the creative contributions from the rest of the cast and crew squandered by having been labelled – tacitly but unambiguously – 'uncreative'. It's worth noting here that the incorporation model elegantly minimises this danger.

I don't know if this is still the case, but in the past one never saw IBM delivery vehicles: well, delivery vehicles with 'IBM' written on the sides. I asked an IBM executive, why? "Because we're not a logistics company." Fair enough. IBM bought in logistics when it needed them. They were using the clustering model in which a company purchases another company's expertise and resources not available in-house. Fine for delivery vans; any good for creativity?

Apparently: yes. Clustering is the model that keeps many advertising agencies, architectural companies, lawyers' chambers, groups of musicians, and small accountancy or auditing practices, afloat. Its main advantage is that the management of these predominantly creative small organisations can be specifically geared for the effective management of creative people, without the problem of divisive elites seen in the demarcation system.

The cluster model has one other major advantage: the company buying-in its creativity doesn't have to worry about not being good at, or knowing much about, creativity. One major disadvantage is that the company doesn't have to worry about not being good at, or knowing much about, creativity. Simultaneously an advantage and disadvantage. You make computers and your customers are unlikely to be concerned that you don't know much about delivering them; as long as they arrive. But if yours is a company whose products are to ooze creativity, will your clients be equally content that you've decided to leave all that stuff to others, perhaps even having delegated responsibly for judging whether it's any good or appropriate for use in your products?

Even if you reserve the cluster solution only for particularly arcane creative tasks, it is essential that your company retains high expertise in knowing how best to communicate with the external creatives. The company that boasts of its creative products can't afford to abdicate all knowledge of how creativity is initiated, progressed, managed and evaluated. This is knowledge that is hard to acquire – and then keep fresh – within a company otherwise overwhelmingly content with the management of colleagues perceived as not creative.

The last option, describing a relationship between company and creative, is segregation. Here, self-employed creatives – therefore not employees of clustering companies – offer their expertise for temporary hire or commission. They may be fine-artists, musicians, novelists, poets or even creativity experts. They differ from their closely related colleagues in clusters by having decided that their personal creative goals are paramount, of greater importance to them than a reliable income as part of a clustered company more willing than they are to adapt its creativity to the needs of a client.

Segregation is great if a client commissions a portrait, but it'll be the artist who signs the completed canvas as his or her work. 'Segregational' creatives are happy to apparently sell their creativity, but it's generally on their own terms.

So, all four of Davis and Scase's options for obtaining creativity have their weaknesses: incorporation risks infecting creatives with extrinsic concerns; demarcation sets up divisive elites and devalues the creativity of others; clustering encourages the company to become dangerously ignorant and insensitive to the creativity it relies upon; and segregation places its creativity in the hands of people more interested in their own goals than those of the company. Oh dear, what's best to do?

As a general rule, I suggest the following...

- Avoid the segregation option of self-employed creators until you need a portrait of your retiring chairperson or a fanfare for the arrival of the next one.

- Use specialist cluster services only when the project is beyond the scope of your in-house creative expertise, but, even then, make sure that your company's hard-won and high-level skills in managing creatives are used when interacting with the external cluster company.

- Adopt as a default solution a combination of the demarcation and incorporation models. Although apparently contradictory in their use of creative colleagues, the best bits of each can be combined and the bad elements discarded. The strength of demarcation is the phenomenally rich range of positive management interventions it encourages, all aimed at activating the deepest possible creativity from colleagues. Its weakness is elitism. The power of incorporation is its anti-elitism; its weakness is its reluctance to use management techniques specifically honed for creativity.

My suggestion therefore is that a wise company, eager for creativity, should use incorporation as its basic structuring model whilst ensuring that project/account managers know and use the specialist skills associated with demarcation to respect, nurture and sometimes protect the work of the creatives within the team. If this works, the creatives will create to their best ability and others aren't excluded or labelled uncreative; for any sparks of their creativity can quickly be seen and fanned by a knowledgeable, skilful and alert manager.

NOW!
"WHY HANG AROUND?"

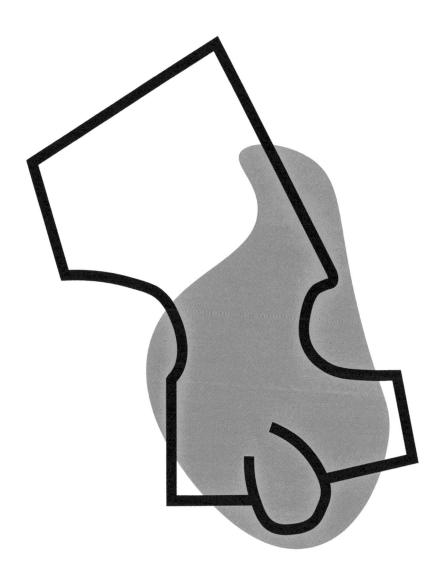

Now! is your colleague who can energise the dullest project, but she is also your impulsive colleague who acts without thinking first.

Now! is your inspirational colleague, the antidote to your department's habitual over-thinking, but she's also your annoying colleague who steamrollers you into key tasks of her latest unplanned scheme.

Now! is your valuable colleague who brings sparkling creativity to the department, but she's also an absolute liability and, frankly, the sooner she goes the better.

Do you work with a Now!? I once did. A creative colleague joined, in a senior position, the organisation I then led. He was fantastic, hoovering up work and erupting an endless stream of good ideas. I was so proud at my HR ability in hiring him. Problem: no one could work with him. Whilst displaying characteristics of several of the creative caricatures I've sketched in this book, the dominant trait that quickly emerged was similar to my fictitious Now! in that he not only demanded immediate – and sometimes unnecessary – work of himself, but also expected immediate responses from others, regardless of their own priorities and preferred ways of working. This was acceptable for a time, with the help of some supportive and sympathetic words from line-managers and repeated attempts on my part to moderate his demands. Alas, no good: he was, as far as I could see, irredeemably Now!

I wondered whether we were simply experiencing a clash of cultures, for my new senior colleague had held – in retrospect, a worryingly large number of – managerial jobs in industries more commercially focused than mine. Were we simply – and perhaps usefully – being offered an alternative way of working? I tried again to oil the gears that connected my Now! to the dominant culture of my organisation. No good. I had therefore either to attempt to change the preferred working practices of an entire stratum of my business to accommodate Now! or try to adjust my new colleague's view of how collaborative work is best carried out. I decided against attempting the former and again failed with the latter option. So, regretfully, and in consultation with senior colleagues, I decided that the value of his hard work and creative ideas was outweighed by the damage he was doing to the outputs of other colleagues through his requirement for them to service his immediate needs. He left.

I entirely accept that the raw creativity of my real life Now! should have been better protected by me as his ultimate manager whilst I was, at the same time, protecting his colleagues. I recognise, only now and too late, that I failed in my 'translation' work as a creative Facilitator.

Let me retreat from painful reality to the caricature Now! and suggest ways in which her manager can act.

Now!s can be inspirational and charismatic. Successful politicians often have a dab of Now! in their psychological make-up bag resulting in popular success way beyond actual ability. In a company Now! might, therefore, be very useful in attracting new clients and energising a sleepy project team. She could also be a refreshing corrective to ponderous planning; useful when a fresh and energetic eye is needed to spot the solution to an old, apparently intractable, problem.

It's just annoying and unprofessional how she commits herself and others to actions without adequate consultation; and it's galling to feel pressured to go along with her spontaneity even though you know its dangers lie unconsidered in the wake of her warp-speed. But if you hold firm and refuse to comply, you're the departmental 'old-guard-fuddy-duddy'.

One strategy for managing Now! not even worth considering is trying to change her into a careful, punctilious colleague: it's just not going to work. Instead, it's best to focus on her positive attributes whilst minimising the effect of negative traits. So, assign her to urgent but straightforward projects that require immediate action, or to accounts on which your clients are always changing their minds. Clients' vacillations would annoy most of your creative colleagues but could be read positively by Now! as opportunities for further creativity. Perhaps you have a particularly sleepy team? Try assigning Now! to it on the 'breath of fresh air' principle, but not to an already effective but pedantic team in the hope that they will pin her down; it will end in tears all round.

Now! will probably be effective when working alone. She'll feel liberated from others' apparent pedantry. You will probably need stoutly to defend the perimeter of her lava field, but, within its confines, her volcanic creativity might be valuable to you for as long as you consider it safe. When in a team, she will enjoy working with Playful, but will loath Picky and probably – but less so – Artiste. Her feelings will be reciprocated. Now!'s personal goal may well be to set up her own business; you can imagine the fireworks of its early months. You might consider whether the quality of her creative ideas at work is worth your trying to dissuade her from this ambition.

Colleagues of Now! should be sure to assert their own needs. Unless unusually perceptive, they may initially be bowled over by her energy and fall-in with her ill-considered plans; but as reality dawns they shouldn't hesitate to say: "That's all very well Now! but you haven't considered the implications of that idea." She won't like it, but your organisation probably needs it to be said. Wise colleagues will confide in their manager if they think Now!'s impetuosity is damaging to the organisation.

PROJECT BRIEFS, TASK ALLOCATION AND DIVERSE NON-CONFORMISTS

Chapter 12 *Courageous companies: creative chaos*, set out crucial roles of managers of colleagues involved with projects requiring significant creativity. It stressed their vital role in translating organisational imperatives into language and action from which creativity can grow. Two common elements to pass through this process are the project brief and the assignment of colleagues to particular tasks. Chapter 12 also stressed the importance of a diverse workforce if deep creativity is to emerge. The current chapter expands on these three points: project briefs, task allocation and diverse non-conformists.

Project Briefs

From my earlier descriptions of the unstructured – even chaotic – soil in which creativity grows best, you might conclude that the goals a manager receives from a client or from head office, might need to be translated into a project brief as vague as possible to allow the creative mind freedom to explore 'the maze'. The maze bit of this assumption is right; 'vague' is wrong, for precision is needed, but only around the edges.

A manufacturing company is worried that the new toy in development is too similar to the products of competitors. It tells the creatives' manager: "Get them to paint it fluorescent orange and make it flash." So the ineffective manager duly briefs his or her creative colleague: "Paint it fluorescent orange and make it flash." The effective manager, who understands creativity, says: "Make it stand out on the shelf."

The lesson here is to define in the brief what is needed, not how it is achieved. The first manager dangles only extrinsic reward to the creative who will promptly leave the maze at exit one having grumpily done exactly what he or she was ordered to do. The second manager has sensibly translated head office's apparently hyper-precise demand into 'make it stand out on the shelf', thus allowing the creative to wander the maze enjoying the intrinsic motivation of creativity, to emerge with an innovative idea at one of its higher-level exits.

Although head-office's diktat was clear – orange and flashing – it was, in reality, not precise. What the company was really concerned about was the similarity of its product to those of other manufactures. 'Orange and flashing' was simply one way of distinguishing it, and, if its competitor's toys were also orange and flashing, not a very sensible way. Far more articulate would have been a simple: "We're worried it'll look too much like the others." Briefs should be extremely precise, but only around their edges. Leave the inside to be filled with creativity.

Imagine you're Count Franz Oppersdorff: a rich music lover living in Silesia in the early nineteenth-century. Easy. "Hi

Beethoven! I'd like to commission a new symphony from you; for performance next year please."

Beethoven knows what a symphony is: a standard number of movements; established classical structure for each movement; an accepted way of moving through keys and developing material. "Yeah fine," he replies, "...sure, I'll write one for you. Five hundred florins: half now, the rest when it's finished."

You've given your creative a good brief by clearly communicating what you want and agreeing the resources needed: time and money. Additionally, you've avoided the 'orange and flashing' trap by wisely not attempting to instruct Beethoven on what to do inside his symphony. You've resisted telling him: "It's got to have tunes I can hum." or "It mustn't last longer than twenty minutes." You know this is not your business; it's for the creative to decide, not you. But perhaps, ruefully, you reflect that if you did know how to do all that music stuff, you'd write the thing yourself and save five hundred florins.

And so, Beethoven sets – eventually – to work in a maze tingling with the intrinsic motivation that his wise patron has awarded him. There, free from gagging extrinsic motivations, he sets about bending – almost to breaking point – all those conventions, traditions and 'rules' of the nineteenth-century symphony, emerging from the creative maze with his fifth symphony. You know its first movement: it starts da da da dooooo. Not much of a tune at all; but great!

A final example of the helpfully empty project brief concerns Michelangelo's frescos in the Sistine Chapel. In line with the common practice of Renaissance Rome, his patron, Pope Julius II, almost certainly defined the subject matter to be depicted in the ceiling's painting; a plan the artist ignored. This refusal of Michelangelo to allow his patron to dictate content is usually seen as a sign of the high opinion the artist held of himself. But could it also articulate his perhaps intuitive understanding that the deepest creativity must be free from constraint?

So, in summary, I can do no better than quote Amabile on the subject of defining project briefs that promote – rather than constrain – creativity: 'Present a clear strategic direction for projects... but allow as much operational autonomy as possible to employees in the day-to-day carrying out of their projects.'

Task Allocation

Hotel folklore has it that there is a pastry chef at the London Ritz who prepares just one kind of dessert. It's superb. He's the master of that single pudding. Perfect every time; utterly unchanging.

And I know for a fact that there is a piano builder working at the Steinway factory in Hamburg, Germany, who just makes the hammer that hits the C# string two octaves above middle C. He told me: "Yeah, management once asked me to move on to making E. Tried it for a bit, but it wasn't the same." And it wasn't the same because, indeed, it wasn't the same.

Craft: admirable, skilful, perhaps meditative, satisfying, a useful activity; but craft, not significant creativity. The results of the chef and the Steinway craftsman are splendidly determined, perfect and, perhaps of necessity, perfectly predictable.

But significant creativity thrives on challenge and the excitement of novelty; it relishes the risks of indeterminacy rather than the certainty of determinacy. So, would it be sensible to get a creative person to do the same thing over and over again? Obviously not: they'd get bored and not do it so well. A craftsperson would be much better.

You are the manager of Jane. She created that marketing campaign for your company's phenomenally successful range of upmarket household paints called *Colour my Castle*. You want to relaunch it now with high-gloss as well as emulsion and normal gloss finishes. Who do you give the brief to? Jane? She was brilliant last time. I'm certain many managers would do just that.

But to creative Jane, it's insufficiently challenging and not new. She has therefore got low creative motivation for this project; and even that's extrinsic in that she's got to be commercially successful again. The best she will probably come up with is a 'maze exit one' solution: *Colour my Shiny Castle*.

If a company requires significant innovation, it needs the creative to gestate new ideas that diverge from, even challenge, the status quo. These ideas are, by their very nature, unpredictable. As with Schrödinger's imperilled quantum cat: put a creative on the job and you don't really know what you're getting until you've got it!

Companies often claim to welcome indeterminate, divergent creativity; but I suspect that comparatively few really do. Like 'green-washing' for easy environmental credit, 'creativity-washing' is common. If *100 Great Vegetarian Recipes* sold well, then the publishers are highly likely to commission *100 Great Vegan Recipes* and ignore that new colleague sitting in the corner who suggests *100 Great Excuses to Avoid a Vegan Dinner Party*.

The discovery of penicillin is sometimes said to have come about by accident, but this isn't quite true. Alexander Fleming was actively looking for a way of killing bacteria. The only 'accident' was that he left some bacteria-infected petri dishes in his lab before going away on holiday, only to find on his return, mould growing around the bacteria. If that had been me, I would have sworn a bit about more perfectly good bacteria samples being ruined and would have washed the mould away. But he – and this is the key point – was open to a divergent creative idea that allowed him to notice that the bacteria were being killed by the mould. And the mould was penicillin: the world's first antibiotic. So, his creativity wasn't a random accident or just lucky, but was based on Fleming's knowledge of bacteria; not restricted to a reliable craft skill but expanded by creative divergence into new knowledge of inestimable value.

I'm here, not denigrating craft or the craftsperson, merely underlining – perhaps a little brutally – the different position on the creativity spectrum they inhabit. But craft is a vehicle of creativity and can prompt significant creativity. Perhaps the Ritz chef will one day try a different ingredient and a new dish will emerge. Perhaps the Steinway technician will say to his manager: "Can we try changing the kind of felt we use for the C# hammer? I think it'll sound better."

Chapter 22 *Creativity in your R&D department* expands on the intimate relationship between craft and creativity.

Diverse non-conformists

Creativity involves change. Change is – at least to some extent – non-conforming. Creativity is, therefore, non-conforming. Well yes, I suppose this is logically true. But the evolution of the UK's TV programme *Strictly Come Dancing* into *Strictly Come Dancing, The Results Show* is hardly a shinning banner for the power of creativity. But I've tied my wagon to the controversial 'spectrum' view of creativity, ranging from barely creative problem-solving to Michelangelo. So, I reluctantly have to accept that the person who came up with…*The Results Show* was exercising creativity, albeit of bovine quality.

But is *The Results Show* non-conformist to any significant extent? No. Evolutionary, yes I suppose so, but in the same amateur league of creativity as the console-game *Fifa Football Manager 2021* becoming *Fifa Football Manager 2022*. Is this the limit of creative innovative thought your organisation is looking for from its creative colleagues, a barely discernible non-conformity of irrelevant divergence from the status quo?

So, we sigh in despair at these predictable minuscule creative baby-steps, which tediously confirm mundane expectations; while we wish for a blast of challenging non-conformist divergence. Of course we do, because we're hugely in favour of non-conformity, right? Let's listen to the enthusiastic ways we often describe our non-conforming colleagues at work.

"He's totally off the wall!" rather than the positive summary of the same person: "He's really different!" What about: "She's not really one of us..." as opposed to: "She's a breath of fresh air!"? Here are some more pairings reflecting a popular rejection of non-conformist divergence, followed by a much rarer, positive welcoming of its appearance.

"She just doesn't get it!" / "She's got such a different take on things."

"Nobody knows where he's coming from." / "He brings new ideas."

"That idea will never work!" / "She's got real determination."

"She's a round peg in a square hole." / "Maybe she's right…"

"He won't last long!" / "We could do with a shake up!"

"She's got to buckle down!" / "Great that she asks 'why?' so often."

It is not hard to decide which column of comments is the more useful for promoting divergent, non-conforming creativity. It's true that non-conformity is challenging to many people, but, if – as I have argued – significant creativity is often accompanied by, and frequently rooted in, non-conformity, then the managers of an organisation relying on the creativity of colleagues would be wise to welcome and encourage its challenging presence: perhaps, at least, by modelling the use of second column epithets.

SUMMARY

To strengthen creativity, managers of creatives should:

- ensure that each project brief is clear about the aim but allows the creative freedom to dream up the way the aim is met

- assign tasks to creatives that are new, exciting, challenging and free of extrinsic motivators

- be sceptical of slothful evolution

- promote an atmosphere that welcomes, rather than fears, the divergent non-conformity of creatives.

YOU

"ME¿ CREATIVE? WELL, JUST LET ME THINK..."

This chapter isn't about a single creative person. There is no new colleague here for Wobbly or Artiste. Instead, it's about you. It's about your discovering what kind of creative you are. And it's also about how useful this self-knowledge is when you're working with your creative colleagues.

If you've already read some of the creative caricatures sketched here, you'll almost certainly have been reminded of some of your own work colleagues: Playful, childlike rather than childish; and Solo, who doesn't like teamwork; as well as Wobbly, the nervous one; and Artiste, who can't take criticism; and there are the others too. All creative and all useful to a company that values the creativity of its colleagues; but a bit tricky to work with from time to time. But did you recognise yourself in any of them? In some of them? All of them?

Whilst working on each of their chapters I found some of the caricatures easier to draw than others. I was puzzled by this at first but then realised that the ones I found easier were those with whom I personally identified most closely. So, Artiste was comparatively hard for me to describe for I've never found criticism difficult to take. Solo was easy to draw, for I – like him – prefer to work alone. And Playful was straightforward too, because I also can be a bit Playful at times: the informality of the Working With Creatives logo or maybe the tone of this book, perhaps gives that game away. I think I'm a combination of at least three or four of the caricatures. How many reminded you of you? Which were they? Are you surprised, even shocked? And, perhaps even more importantly, has this new knowledge made you reassess what you are like to work with as a colleague?

The point here is that it really helps to know your own creative styles if your goal is to work more happily with colleagues, having understood their creative styles. Manage to do this and you stand a better chance of harmonious matches. Concentrate solely on your colleague whilst ignoring your own creative-self, and the professional relationship is more likely to be dissonant; generally not a useful goal.

I asked if more than one of the sketches seemed a bit like you. I suppose some people might just have one creative pose – a Wobbly or a Monk perhaps – but in my experience most creatives are a complicated mixture of several. Do you also recall that some of the chapters have mentioned similarities between caricatures? I said, for example, that Artiste seemed to be Wobbly's sister and also predicted potential conflicts: Picky and Playful was one, their incompatible personalities seldom working effectively together.

The conclusion to draw from this is that if you recognise – and know how to handle – your colleague's styles of creativity, whilst at the same time understanding your own, it should be possible, temporarily, to adjust your own balance of styles to complement better those you've perceived in a tricky co-worker. Perhaps you've always found that person in product development challenging to work with. Is it really just the way he never does up his cuff buttons and starts every sentence with "So…", or is it that you're approaching him with a creative style incompatible – dissonant – with his? The next section of this chapter illustrates some of this theory in practical scenarios based on the isolated personality traits that my creative caricatures represent. First, they are simplified here, for easy reference.

Picky enjoys the process of creativity more than getting to the product of that creativity: "Well, I understand your point, narrator, but it's just that everything must be perfect. So the process mustn't be rushed."

Molotov, the revolutionary, fights for change: "It's management that's the problem!"

Artiste thinks there is no distinction between herself and her creative work: "Yes, I know I can be a bit touchy at times but I can't stand other people trying to take over my projects with their smart suggestions. It's so wounding!"

Playful at work looks like a child at play: "How can I be creative if I have to pretend to be a boring old manager?"

Fibber's creativity is bound up with fiction: "Some people have even accused me of lying! But, well, that's not really fair. No, not really, but…"

Wobbly feels professionally insecure: "I love my job and I get paid for doing it; can my luck hold, especially with the management we've got here? They really don't understand us creatives at all!"

Facilitator's creativity is evidenced through the creativity of others: "I get real satisfaction from seeing my creativity at the roots of others' projects."

Monk's commitment is to his creativity not his employer: "'It's my company's duty to provide me with the tools to do what I was born to do. That's all there is to it."

Solo is very creative but hopeless in teams: "I just need to see things through from start to finish. What's wrong with that?"

Now! is impulsive: "Why hang around?"

You:
(You fill in the objective overview and the subjective quotation!)

If-Only is good at excuses: "I could do something really special if only they would let me!"

Examples of naturally consonant professional relationships between creative colleagues might include Fibber and Molotov, for both are on a mission. Molotov forges ahead, whilst Fibber provides the narrative/propaganda that justifies and explains – sometimes with enhanced truth – the revolutionary changes planned or already underway. Interactions between the two will remain creatively productive, as long as they continue to share the same mission and strategy.

A second relationship that shouldn't require too much adjustment of preferred working style on either part is that between Facilitator and Picky. Facilitator will commonly set up various opportunities for Picky's precision to inspect. This will probably continue quite smoothly until Facilitator's pragmatic sense of progress requires her to point out to her colleague that a conclusion has to be achieved at some defined point. This may cause a rift that Facilitator, rather than Picky, is better equipped to address: perhaps through pointing out the many opportunities Picky will have for detailed scrutiny beyond their current project.

Now! and Playful is another pair of creatives who are likely to enjoy working together, as long as they can agree on which game to play. Similarly, Monk and Molotov – both driven by higher ideals – will get on fine for as long as they want to change the same thing. But what would happen if two Wobbly's work together? It would certainly be a consonant professional relationship but hardly a psychologically secure atmosphere for creativity.

More pertinent to the ambition of this chapter are those relationships that are intrinsically rather dissonant, but which, with knowledge and flexibility by at least one participant, can be nudged into consonance. Below, Playful and Solo exemplify this positive transition. They find themselves about to start work on a project together. Their unmoderated, dissonant interaction is summarised by this imaginary dialogue…

Playful: So, the project needs all of us to work as a team? It'll
           be fun!
Solo: Well, you can count me out then.

A Solo who understands both his own solitary preference and
the gregarious nature of Playful, might be able to moderate his
dismissive response whilst still insisting on his own basic creative
strategy…

Playful: So, the project needs all of us to work as a team? It'll
           be fun!
Solo: Yeah, I can see that; and some of its elements are
           really important to me. I'll be of most use if you get
           me in for them.

Here, Facilitator and Monk are at the same early stage of their
shared project…

Facilitator: We need to be pragmatic about all this.
Monk: So any ideals are out of the window before we start!

This would have been the dissonant interaction, but Monk is able
to make a helpful adjustment without compromising the root of
his own creativity…

Facilitator: We need to be pragmatic about all this.

Monk: Yes, I can see that down the road a bit; but we've got to be able to show some real changes quickly to keep people onside.

Molotov and Picky...

Molotov: Right! Well. we've got to get that changed at once!

Picky: But you haven't got a Gantt chart yet!

Becomes...

Molotov: Right! Well, we've got to get that changed at once!

Picky: Yes, as soon as possible. I can do a careful plan to help it happen.

For all their crudity, these examples suggest that predictably dissonant interactions with colleagues at work can be made more positive with thought, based on understanding of both your own and your colleague's motivations to creativity. Subsequent moderation of what is said can then produce a mutually creative environment.

But, earlier in this chapter, I pointed out that your real-life creative colleague is unlikely to be an incarnate version of just one of my single-faceted caricatures. He or she is likely, at times, to display features from many within – and beyond – my limited cast of creatives. The first set of dialogues I offered showed naturally harmonious pairs of creatives whilst the second set presented other, trickier pairings, pointing to the possibility of moderating responses in order to decrease natural dissonance. I have reminded you that real-life creative colleagues will often possess more than just one spur to their creativity and will therefore display a variety of characteristics in their professional life. Could these three observations: multifaceted reality, the possibility of harmony, and moderating dissonance; be fused? I am here suggesting an opportunity for managers and colleagues to dip into their own repertoire of creative spurs to bring out the one that is the most likely to be consonant with that being projected by his or her colleague. Look back at the three 'moderated' responses. The first sees Solo using some of his inner Artiste to give a harmonious response to Playful. In the second, Monk is able to find aspects of Molotov and Now! in his repertoire with which to ensure a positive dialogue with Facilitator, whilst Picky successfully deploys some of her usually hidden Facilitator to set up a positive working relationship with Molotov.

Being skilled at identifying the current flavour of creativity that your colleague is exhibiting and then being able to match it to an appropriate flavour from your own repertoire of creative behaviours is a managerial and collegiate accomplishment both rare and very useful. Rare indeed, but it can be learned. As long as the prerequisites are in place: the ability to identify the kind of creative you're faced with; the knowledge of how best to respond; an understanding of your own combination of creative personality types; and skill at selecting the appropriate one to deploy.

But surely this summary of 'how to do it' is massively simplistic. Human relationships – even professional relationships – don' t succeed simply by consciously dialling-in the correct response to the message you've just received. To pretend that a few caricatures give you the full range of answers is clearly ridiculous. True, but that's not what I'm claiming. The ideas I've outlined here do not pretend to be sufficient, but they are necessary for excellent colleagues and managers who do not have an instinctive gift for always being able to work happily and effectively with creatives. Such people do exist – I once worked for one – but they turn hens' teeth into a common commodity. The rest of us have to learn a bit, practise a bit and think a bit.

CREATIVITY IN YOUR R&D DEPARTMENT

Creativity and craft

This chapter examines intersections within your research and development (R&D) department connecting creativity, craft, time and applause. First, a reminder that Chapter 4 *Definitions and characteristics* argued that the product of creativity will have both novelty and utility if it is to deserve being called 'creative'. In other, less laden, words: it's got to be both new and useful.

But creativity can't be seen to exist at all if it is not expressed through some endeavour; and that endeavour probably resides within the context of a strongly associated craft. The craft of joinery, for example, advises its members how to join pieces of wood together; the craft of horticultural design has views on building a garden; philosophy can help you think about good and evil; the accumulated wisdom of hydrology will have views on how to build an irrigation system; and so on. I am not referring to formal traditional craft guilds with explicit signed-up members, but to a concept of a craft that informally promulgates its generally accepted understanding of how work within its discipline is best carried out.

Crafts generally exert a cohesive, rather than disruptive, influence on their creative members and on the creatives' audiences, clients, and employers. From this point, I'll simply call this trio the 'audience'. And, crucially, the craft owns the criteria against which the quality of creativity is judged within its confines. All this gives the impression that crafts are static, conservative entities resistant to change. Although this may seem to be true, times change, fashions evolve, fresh technologies demand change and new, preferred ways of working inevitably nudge any craft interested in its own future, to evolve. So, within architecture, for example, we have seen the craft skills of the drawing board replaced by the new skills of computer-aided design.

In Chapter 2 *Are we all creative?* I used the phrase 'craft creativity' to distinguish it from 'significant creativity', suggesting that craft skills inform the lower – not particularly creative – end of the creativity spectrum: the end that looks, at best, for evolutionary, rather than revolutionary, change. Fine; but in this chapter I'm adding a more obviously honourable interpretation of its role, for it provides the roots of most – if not all – creative endeavours. I'm suggesting that the 'craft' of a discipline sets its foundations by bringing together, in a respected canon, its generally accepted purposes, goals, ways of working and evaluative criteria. The craft neither promotes nor constrains creativity but provides the channel through which whatever creativity exists can be expressed. An example: I'm familiar with the craft of writing in English; so was Shakespeare. We use the same craft. The only trifling difference is that he has used it to communicate a somewhat higher degree of creativity than I can quite manage.

So, the craft provides a reservoir of received wisdom, probably accumulated from many generations of practitioners who communicated their varying degrees of creativity through that particular craft. At the problem-solving end of the creativity spectrum, the wisdom of the craft is extremely useful in giving modestly creative members the basic skills necessary for solutions to frequently seen problems with known solutions. Higher up the spectrum, the craft still provides the subject's outer framework but is – one hopes – increasingly silent on 'solutions': those are the responsibility of the creative person speaking through the craft.

Your R&D department and craft

Many companies have R&D departments within which creative colleagues work on projects typically ranging from those that are tightly defined and whose outcomes are predictable and required, to others that are seen as 'blue-skies': speculative and uncertain in their result, timescale, cost and usefulness. It is easy to see why many companies are prepared to invest in the creativity of the former, for both newness and usefulness are pretty much assured, whilst the blue-sky costs come with doubts about... well, everything.

So, basic but very useful 'crafts skills' almost certainly dominate the work of the R&D department. This is what I call 'craft R&D'. As craft frames the consensual, problem-solving regions of the creativity spectrum, the R&D focus here is also on continuity, albeit enriched by a little gentle evolution.

Craft R&D is based on an accepted status quo, not only in what is to be achieved but also on a knowledge and acceptance of the ways in which that desired creative outcome should and can be found. Craft R&D is reliable in that its results are not only likely to be achieved, but also loudly applauded and this is because they are evaluated by their audience within the same craft context that nurtures their emergence. The craft-based creative and his or her audience are therefore 'on the same page'. The creative work has successfully stretched, but not fundamentally challenged, the established craft, and its audience has duly applauded, secure in an evaluation based on a shared understanding of the craft. It's the way most useful and new – therefore creative – developments happen. For instance, the computer I am typing this book on is great, albeit just a predictable and assured development of the one I consigned to the tip last year.

I've argued that applause for craft R&D creativity comes about easily because all concerned in the process share compatible understandings of, and respect – even fondness – for, the established craft. Indeed, when applauding a successful outcome of a craft R&D project, the audience of managers is probably linked to the project by a shared understanding of: the problem the project solved; the minor innovations that were needed; the market conditions into which the solution was to be launched; and the assessment criteria likely to be applied by the new product's likely purchasers. Of course a satisfactory result will lead to applause.

So, there is likely to be a comfortable harmony linking the competent craft R&D creative to his or her audience. Not so for his or her blue-sky colleague. Here, the uncertain and speculative nature of creativity predicts a discontinuity that separates the creative from the expectations of his or her audience. The creative has wandered off-piste, or at least closer to the edges of the traditions, established practices and goals of their craft. The audience is likely to be left bewildered by a newness that they find impossible to evaluate – and therefore applaud or boo – given the normative evaluation criteria built into the rules of the craft: rules that they still follow as their guide to recognising quality in creativity.

Usefulness

There's a popular TV show in the UK at the moment (2022) that shows the presenter hanging around municipal dumps watching people throwing away their unwanted possessions: old cupboards, tables, lamps, beds; anything really. As my fellow citizens heave their rubbish into vast skips yawning below them, the presenter, eagle-eyed, prepares to pounce on a favoured object. After a brief chat with its owner, she inevitably gets them to agree to give her their 'rubbish' which she then takes back to her workshop, turns into up-cycled treasure, sells for a fortune, and donates the profit to charity. I expect you have similar shows. They're a sub species of the classic 'before and after'/'horror to big reveal' trope of contemporary 'feel-good' TV. I love it.

Yes, an example of a TV cliché, but more interesting than most; for rather than simply contrasting hideous 'before' and elegant 'after' it's also a meditation on utility. And 'utility' – or near synonyms – was one of the keywords spotted in most of those definitions of creativity discussed in Chapter 4 *Definitions and characteristics*. So, back at the tip: what was useless to the old owner becomes useful to the presenter.

So, if 'utility' was one of only two essential properties that define creativity, the other being 'novelty', it follows, if you accept the definition, that the loathed but interesting table teetering on the edge of the skip has had a traumatic creative journey during its life and that there's more to come. When it was first sold, it was presumably useful; and, due to its unique design, it was also novel. Utility and novelty; it embodied the creativity of its maker. But now its current owner has no use for it, and so cannot now value it as 'creative'. But its new TV-presenter owner can, for it is useful to her as a novel up-cycling challenge; a conclusion shared by its eventual purchaser and certainly by me in front of my screen.

It seems that pinning the label 'This is an expression of creativity' to an object, a process, an idea… is subjective and susceptible to revision over time.

Time

I have already said that crafts, although essentially conservative, do change over time, usually in more or less grudging response to increasing pressure from members at the higher ends of the creativity spectrum, itchy within its current traditions. The following section looks at the implications for creatives of this time-based process.

To understand the examples set out below, it's useful to know that my own field of musicology uses shorthand tags such as baroque, classical and romantic to loosely – very loosely – summarise a time period's preferred way of composing serious music. The tags define the craft of musical composition of that era, and these change over time. So baroque conventions gradually shifted to classical practices, and these later morphed into what are termed romantic ways of composing, reacting to, and contemplating music. The craft of musical composition was, and is, always changing, and this craft isn't unique. The same holds true for fine art, but also for the crafts of accountancy, town planning, the travel industry, medicine and, actually, for every human endeavour. Endeavours inevitably form crafts, and changing tastes and technologies demand that crafts evolve over time.

Creatives express their creativity through endeavours; they therefore work within a craft. Members who are significantly creative will often be in the frontline pushing the craft – through their work – to evolve. If enough of them push for similar developments, the craft will change.

But now for some examples relating all that theory to practice.

If, as a creative person, you'd like professional respect and commercial success whilst still alive, the most important thing you should do is ensure you're born at the right time. Aim to get your first mature flowering of creativity to coincide with the conventions of your craft being happily settled but still capable of significant innovation, before they break apart under the pressure of impatient, probably younger, highly creative members. You've managed it: you are W. A. Mozart, born when classicism was starting to reach maturity and considered it had all the answers. A secure craft. Okay, I know that Mozart died penniless, but that was his own fault, not caused by his style of composition deserting his craft.

But perhaps you are born just a bit late. If so, you'll inherit an admirably sophisticated craft that lays out cogently and comprehensively all the tenets of your trade, but which still leaves some scope, if not for massive innovation, then at least for the final developments that bring the craft to perfection. These will be new creative embellishments of already established principles, or perhaps the final working out in practice of long-considered theories. The trouble comes as you get old and a bit proud of your supreme expertise in your craft, for now you'll almost certainly be faced with a hard choice: stay doing what you're so good at doing and risk being called an old-fogey whose work is increasingly forgotten, or, take a deep breath and jump into the worryingly chastening water of the new ideas springing up around you. Your name is J. S. Bach and you worked towards the end of the baroque craft of musical composition. And you stuck with it, impervious to the new craft of classicism gradually rendering you redundant.

But perhaps your birth timing is just a bit off, but at the other end, and you carelessly get yourself born a bit too early so that you hit creative maturity at the fag-end of one established set of craft skills but before its replacement has been worked out. Now you have a real creative job on your hands, for you'll probably have to prove to potential employers – still enjoying the good old days – that you can work creatively within that fading craft tradition whilst at the same time urging the craft to evolve into something more to your youthful taste. But that's not all, for not only do you have to help create the new craft, you also have to demonstrate your mastery of it if you want to get one of the new progressive jobs. What's your name?

You are Claudio Monteverdi and you've just composed a setting of the Vespers for Venice and it's 1610. You need that job at St Mark's and the Vespers is your application letter: 'Listen, you want old renaissance style? I give you old renaissance style; but this next bit? So new: so baroque!' You won't be surprised to learn that I've just invented that quotation from Claudio. The word 'baroque' wasn't used in this context until 1888 and he died in 1643! What is true though is that Claudio wasn't alone in pushing his craft towards what was to become known as the baroque era. I've already suggested in my theory paragraphs that such developments take place as a result of several highly creative craft members all sensing a similar need for change. Claudio had influential colleagues: Allegri, Peri and Caccini. Not heard of them? I'm not surprised. Inventing a new language for a craft is hard work and until it's at least partially achieved it is not clear what you can say through it.

Right, I've presented three commercially successful creatives respected by both their peers and, to varying degrees at varying times, fortunate that their audiences shared the same craft-based evaluative criteria that they themselves worked to. So, they received their rightful applause.

Poor old Vincent Van Gogh didn't; and this was, I suspect, because his audience – potential buyers of his paintings – didn't share Vincent's dangerously personal redefinition of the craft of painting. Okay, they did eventually, but too late: he was dead by then. My three composers all managed, whilst still alive, an alignment that allowed their audiences to see the composers' music as 'useful' as well as 'new'. Each benefited from their audiences' understanding of the crafts which they had energised and graced, crafts which formed the conduits through which their creativity could be expressed. Because Vincent's audience could only see his paintings as 'new' and, I suspect, disconcertingly so, they would not have perceived them as 'useful', and so the expression of creativity that they embodied would have reached no further than Vincent's own studio door and his tiny circle of aligned, but impoverished, admirers.

So, the audience has to perceive usefulness for the innovation to be understood as creative. I've explained why this is indeed likely to emerge if both the audience and the creative share an understanding of what the craft, within which both are involved, is fundamentally about. If, on the other hand, the creative is working in more speculative, blue-sky creativity, he or she is very likely to challenge some principles of the craft, thus breaking the continuity of understanding between the creative and his or her audience.

But I said earlier that opinions on usefulness can change. I gave the example of the TV programme that up-cycles rubbish, turning 'useless' into 'useful'. I even suggested that this oscillation might prompt us, if we are having a particularly pedantic and logical day, to synchronise our judgement of creative/not creative with the useful/not useful oscillations of the objects' various owners. This is clearly ridiculous. I know it sounds like a cop-out, but let's consider the inestimable attraction of 'potentially useful'.

When Christopher Cockerell invented the hovercraft in the 1960s, many hailed its arrival as a creative achievement. Entirely understandable: hovercraft were clearly new and useful. There was a time when you could travel from England to France on one, and take your car, too. 'There was a time', but not now. Why not? Well, I learn that it's because they became too expensive to operate, requiring a lot of expensive fuel to get them to actually hover and requiring technology that was expensive to repair and maintain. So, they became very much less 'useful' and are now generally seen in just a few specialist areas of military and rescue work, and as an intriguingly historical way of getting from the UK's town of Portsmouth to the nearby, and equally – so it's reported – backward-looking, Isle of Wight.

If we take a severe reading of the definition of creativity, we should now withdraw our 'creative' judgement of Cockerell's innovations back in the 1960s. But hang on! Before we do that, what if some new and valuable use for hovercraft pops up in the future, just as it did for the old table at the municipal tip? And I've even got an idea for what that might be. What do you think? Hovercraft are really good at travelling over different surfaces, but burn massive amounts of fuel doing it. The only reason for that excessive consumption is gravity: we've got quite a lot of it on earth; the moon far less. So, as lunar exploration resumes, might hovercraft finally become useful again by zipping across the lunar landscape on just a teaspoon of fuel?

Surely all but the most pedantic should see Cockerall's invention as at least 'potentially creative'?

Another example of potential creativity? Consider Nikola Tesla. Several of his inventions concerning electricity are undoubtedly creative, being both new and useful. His later notebooks, however, hint at radical innovations yet to be realised or successfully applied to a particular use: potentially creative.

And one final pair of potentially creativity examples: 3D TV – or have we already got too bored waiting? – and what's your bet for the 'metaverse'?

Of course, having solved one problem I create another: how long does the world have to wait, hopefully grasping a bit of potential creativity before just giving up and consigning it permanently to the rubbish skip? I don't know.

So, what advice might your managers take from this ragbag of ideas linking creativity, craft, time and applause to your R&D department?

SUMMARY

- Don't use the volume of applause as a guide to the value of blue-sky R&D.

   I've discussed that significant creativity challenges the current understanding of the craft through which it is expressed. This is likely to make it hard for employees, managers and customers still working within, and loyal to, the conventional understanding of the craft, to make reliable judgements about the quality of the creative outputs.

- Be patient with 'potential creativity'.

  With the passing of time, new applications emerge turning good ideas in search of a use, into significant creativity. The wise manager will, of course, continually scan the horizon searching for existing and future applications for current 'potentially creative' innovations; and will encourage the birth of such innovations, as yet – and perhaps forever – innocent of a clear use.

- Don't take too much notice of criticism aimed at the more recherché end of your R&D department.

  As craft-based R&D professionals will still be working within the old craft dispensation, they will likely have an inflated appreciation of the 'usefulness' element of the creativity definition; for it is their ticket to the exclusive creatives' departure lounge. It is therefore not surprising that they should glance sceptically over their shoulders at their blue-sky colleagues.

- Don't allow the blue-sky creatives to denigrate the work of craft-based creatives.

  It's easy to imagine significantly creative employees looking disparagingly at their more literally utilitarian creative colleagues. This is unfair: for those towards the modest end of the spectrum are more likely than their blue-sky colleagues to have an immediate and demonstrably useful application for development. They are therefore, paradoxically, more obviously creative than their more speculative colleagues.

- Check that your managerial glasses are fit for purpose.

Managers should risk seeing the world though lenses not included in the standard craft-R&D kit. If management cannot conceive of any possible creative development being useful beyond craft-R&D borders, then the standard utilitarian lens is clearly good enough; albeit in a self-fulfilling prophetic kind of way. But if the possibility of regions existing beyond its current craft horizons is accepted by the manager, then riskier glasses, capable of spotting more speculative, uncertain and unappreciated reaches, must be worn.

- Be aware that your craft is probably changing.

Crafts are dynamic. They evolve when new ways of thinking and acting insist on change. If the craft is healthy, this dynamism is inevitable; the effective R&D manager will be wise to embrace rather than oppose it. He or she may be able to predict general changes in direction by enthusiastically charting the key innovative features seen in the latest work of significantly creative members. If these changes seem to be forming a potential consensus among influential peers, a component of the likely new direction of the craft might have been spotted.

IF-ONLY

"I COULD DO SOMETHING REALLY SPECIAL, IF ONLY THEY
WOULD LET ME!"

Once, I was manager to a creative colleague who brought me a new idea for a course we could offer. It was a fairly good idea, but unlikely to attract many customers and certain to make a loss given the resources he claimed were needed. I encouraged him to keep planning but rethink the resource budget. He came back a couple of weeks later with an even more ambitious programme and an even longer list of expensive essential resources, but with nothing new that might attract more customers. He was desperately enthusiastic and really wanted it to start. I tried again: "It sounds great, but it's just too expensive. Have another think about the features that really are essential or ways we could get more buyers."

As you've made it this far through the book, I hope you're now pounding your desk in anger that I was offering extrinsic motivators by going on about resource costs and income against expenditure: both certain to undermine my colleague's creativity. But I wasn't forcing him to leave 'the maze' early by dangling extrinsic rewards; his creative stage was over and he was straying into implementation. I'll return to this point later in the chapter.

At the next meeting, my innovative colleague arrived with even more Wagnerian plans and costs. I suggested he should run a trial with all the resources he needed but on such a small scale that the certain financial loss could be absorbed. "Give it a go. Let's see what it's like." I expected him to be delighted. No, he wasn't. But he did come back a few days later with news that the experiment wasn't worth doing on that scale; it was all or nothing.

I said: "'Okay, pity. Then it's nothing, I'm afraid." He was cross, but even then, did I sense some relief on his face? His name is If-Only. Is he working for you now?

If so, you'll probably have seen him urging a pet project only to be blocked by managers lacking his vision. So ignorant: if only they would just open their eyes! But, more recently, his luck has turned; it is a smaller idea, which, to his amazement, has got the go-ahead from his manager. Unfortunately, it has now run into the sand for reasons If-Only is happy to explain. But reasons that fail to include the fact that he has not done much actual work on it. No, he's clearly been let down by others: such a missed opportunity for the company; it could have been great! But listen, he's got this new idea, it just needs some buy-in from upstairs and he just knows you'd love working on it too!

And perhaps his new idea, like the last, will be supported; it's got some very attractive features in it, all carefully linked to this year's top priorities from your CEO. So, If-Only is likely to be patted on the head and invited to lead the next stage of planning. But this means work!

We are now at the stage that If-Only will morph into Yes-But, producing countless objections to the planned rollout of the idea. Colleagues new to If-Only will be surprised at his reaction. Those who have worked with him for some time will have seen it all before, bored with the predictable procession of prevarication. His wise manager should at this stage thank If-Only for his potentially good idea and send him off to have some more. The next stage will be left to colleagues more skilled at pragmatic hard work. It will be they who discover whether the idea can grow into usefulness. Consequently, it will be their results that will decide whether If-Only is in fact really a creative: a person able to produce something that has both novelty and utility (See Chapter 4 *Definitions and characteristics*).

Now, only thirty years too late, I can see that this is what should have happened with my real life If-Only, who kept on coming up with ever more expensive – and unchallengeable – ways of implementing his innovative course idea. I should have thanked him, pocketed his idea and passed it to the pragmatists.

If-Only shares some characteristics with Picky. He, like Picky, slows down progress, but their motivations are different. Picky enjoys her creative practice and doesn't want it to stop, whilst If-Only doesn't really want it to move beyond the initial idea; and possibly even that has been designed to appear superficially attractive to conceal its inevitable dead-end. Picky does useful work; If-Only adroitly avoids it. Picky can be useful to your organisation in an annoying quality-assurance kind of a way; If-Only may be useless in an apparently beguiling way.

The effectiveness of the smokescreen he can deploy depends on his degree of charisma – and that is likely to be significant – for If-Only would not have settled upon his high-profile avoidance tactic had it not showed early and repeated signs of success.

Such success is dependent on his ability to garner support from colleagues happy to follow him. If-Only is unlikely to have achieved this support without a significant dollop of charisma.

Charisma draws him closer to another caricature we've already met – Molotov – for she, too, argues for change that is opposed. This vocation, to be successful, is assisted by her charisma. But again, just as with Picky, there's a big difference: Molotov really wants the change she's urging and is prepared to work for it; whilst If-Only's banner proclaiming the same goal is a tactic to preserve stasis. On first meeting, Molotov might well embrace If-Only as a comrade-in-arms, but after that their love affair will wither into disdain from Molotov and defensiveness from If-Only. But both are probably charismatic.

Charisma

This book attempts to say a few useful things about creativity at work: tough enough. It's not now going to plunge in any depth into charismatic leadership: another witheringly elusive subject. Our charismatic If-Only is not, therefore, to get a fair hearing from me. But this is due not only to my ignorance of the subject, but also because I am suspicious of charisma; not of its existence which is undeniable, but of the almost magical power it can exert.

I am also sceptical of the operation of charisma, for it shares the unlikely on/off switch of that other sneakily simple word:

genius. Both suggest either you've got it or you haven't, and this, to me, seems an unlikely deviation from the far more common spectrum-based graduations of other human talents such as kindness, empathy, selfishness, musicality and athleticism.

Another commonly ascribed on/off switch is, of course, 'creativity': either you are creative or you're not; but I hope my discussion and rejection of this view presented in Chapter 2 *Are we all creative?* convinces otherwise by revealing a long spectrum of human creativity.

Another worry I have about charisma is well illustrated by If-Only. His probable ability to enthuse others is quite possibly dishonest; a con-trick to disguise his own lack of creativity, or, at best, a mechanism through which he can unload the hard work within and beyond Amabile's maze onto colleagues dazzled by his charisma.

And it perhaps shouldn't surprise us to meet quite a few creatives at work who are judged by colleagues to be charismatic. A clue as to why this should be was given by Max Weber, the German sociologist, in a lecture in 1917 in which he argued that authority comes from three possible sources:

- 'Tradition', or 'how it's always been'. Example: hereditary monarchies.

- 'Law', or 'belief in the validity of legal statutes and professional competence'. Examples: elected leaders and medical doctors.

- 'Charisma', or 'personal devotion and personal trust in the revelations, heroism or other leadership qualities of an individual'. Examples: prophets; successful wartime heroes; and winning sportsmen and women who have defied both the odds and the establishment.

The quotations above come from Damion Searls' translation of Weber's work listed in *Sources cited*.

Although Weber doesn't explicitly relate charisma to creativity it's not hard to join the dots.

This book has argued that creativity always involves change, sometimes revolutionary change; my Molotov caricature being an extreme expression. Neither of Weber's first two roots of authority – tradition and law – sit happily with revolutionary change. Indeed, the revolutionary could almost be defined as someone fighting against tradition and law. But creativity is nevertheless seen within these authorities albeit tending to operate at the lower, evolutionary end of the creativity spectrum, whilst more intense and challenging levels of creativity/change inhabit its higher regions, closer to revolution. So, a highly creative person who wishes to exercise authority – either for the thrill of its intrinsic power or, more morally, for the greater ability it gives for the implementation of change – will need to use what charisma he or she possesses. The other two vehicles for authority, tradition and law, will probably be inaccessible at least until his or her charismatic authority is firmly established. As an example of this procession of authorities, Napoleon Bonaparte's massive revolutionary charisma got him started to the extent that he could then exert legal authority as the legitimate leader of armies, before his traditional authority as the head of a dynastic line of emperors. Thankfully, most highly creative people do not have domination of Europe as their primary objective and therefore content themselves simply with their charismatic authority, which will last just as long as their perceived exceptional achievements, as radical and successful bringers of change, continue to flow; for good or ill.

So, my advice for working with a charismatic creative exemplified by If-Only, is to be careful of his charisma and peer sceptically through its dazzle before deciding to become his acolyte or remaining his polite but cautious colleague. I suggest the charismatic creative's manager should take time, carefully, to examine what creativity lies, or fails to lie, beyond the glitter, before deciding on the best ways of using his skills. It may be that the manager concludes that the potential creativity of the creative's ideas makes him a valuable, if limited, colleague, or she might, alternatively, decide that he is basically a fraudster, that she has no responsibility for his psychotherapy and that he has no useful contribution to make to her organisation.

CREATIVITY AND CUSTOMERS; STALIN AND INTIMACY

Joseph Stalin seldom pops up on my list of the top ten creative facilitators. But on one subject I'm sympathetic: his views on 'formalism'. Apparently, Jo didn't like complicated, 'formalistic' creativity, and in the early years of the Russian Revolution there was a lot of it about. He preferred, I understand, good old straightforward heroic tunes and stories, to the intricate, introspective 'bourgeois' products of his leading creatives, who displayed in their work too much learning for his egalitarian political taste.

I'm really not certain why we, as a species, often prefer, like Stalin: art that is apparently artless; creativity that appears spontaneous; invention that seems to come from nowhere. Perhaps we like it because we resent being lectured by clever-clogs who have, so obviously, worked it all out. So, Stalin's views on formalism really aren't that unusual. The response of his creatives was either to disguise their erudition or pack some warm clothes for Siberia.

But maybe there's another explanation for our species' preference for apparently spontaneous or improvisatory creativity; one more immediately connected to the creative process itself that launches a new idea out of Amabile's metaphorical maze? A thought-out, formalist product of creativity seems just a bit stale to us, too long out of the maze's oven, too pondered, too manufactured, no longer a fresh expression of the maze's heat and humanity. Maybe we sniff all that 'bourgeois' apparatus of learning, drafting and revision now separating us – the observers – from the fellow human being who first had that creative idea, so innocent of encumbrance.

I once, in a lecture to several hundred bored students, held up a cheap little table I'd bought the week before from Ikea and in the other hand another I'd made from scratch. All those still awake agreed that the Ikea table was better: stronger, lighter, with all its bits fitting perfectly. Mine was weaker, awkwardly heavy and generally a bit thrown together with screws that hadn't gone in quite straight. I asked the students to vote on which they would like to take home. All wanted mine; but why? Well, I suspect for the same reason we like homemade cakes and handmade clothes: our connection with the creative is stronger and unmediated by the anonymity of mass reproduction. The German philosopher Walter Benjamin might have seen this reaction as evidence of the 'aura' he sensed surrounding authentic creative objects, which their mechanically reproduced copies lacked. And don't you, too, find it vaguely repellent to learn from TV programmes showing 'how it's made' that your childhood's favourite home-baked biscuit now starts life in a vast vat of glutenous goo being stirred by paddles that could power an ocean liner? Too much machinery; too much intervention between creative inception and optimistic reception. Too much distance between emotion and me! Oh dear, I didn't realise I was such a fan of Stalin.

And then, there are videos made on handphones by young people for the delight of other young people: at the moment (2022) generally displaying 'cute' cats and apparently hilarious dogs. Hugely popular, crudely made and instantly disposable. Dada without the anarchic intent? No, just a bit of fun. But fun with serious implications: they're quick, they're cheap and unmediated by much thought, planning or editing, and they succeed in carrying the creativity of their authors to their applauding audiences. No need for their creators – unlike Shostakovich under Stalin – to hide their erudition beneath a veneer of popularism. The veneer is all that there is; and it works! But it shouldn't. Well, not according to the professional creatives of children's programmes at major TV and film studios, who have successfully argued that children deserve the same production values in the expression of their creativity as adult audiences. But today's TikTok and YouTube suggest otherwise. Not only are carefully acquired skill, knowledge, resources and ambition unnecessary for the effective communication of creativity, it seems that these qualities – in the hands of now struggling traditional TV – are an obstacle, distancing the creative from his or her audience, and the equivalent of all that machinery separating the homemade biscuit of memory from the mass produced version on the supermarket shelf.

I wanted to buy a wardrobe for my spare bedroom. I went to a local antiques shop; you know, the kind that buys 'any old rubbish and sells the finest antiques'. A friend, who knows the difference, came with me.

"How about this one?" I asked.
"No, it's rubbish." he replied.
"How do you know?"
"It's too perfect."

And what he meant was that its perfection was proof of its mass production and therefore distanced us from any real human engagement with its creator. And what he correctly assumed I wanted was that direct connection. It was therefore indeed 'rubbish' to me. The child enthralled by the video of a cute doggy has, I suggest, a similarly pleasurable connection with the creator of the video, one infinitely more engaging than with the creative director behind the big-budget report on the international dog show. Humans just seem to want to engage with unfiltered creativity.

Take prehistoric cave painting as another example. It seems that when painting their extraordinary art on the walls, some creatives would press a dripping hand against a nearby blank bit. A delighted archaeologist, several thousand years later, always – at least on Discovery Channel – insists on placing his or her own hand on the print and announcing the delicious sense of communication they are experiencing, linking the creator to today's scientist. Okay, the distinguished archaeologist then goes on to speculate on the cultural significance of the actual paintings, but always in a scholarly voice somehow devoid of the intuitive and immediate excitement of touching hands with a human from the past through the product of their ancient creativity.

I like good food and I like good wine. So when holidaying, I choose a destination with both and sit content in a local restaurant eating cheese from the farm across the next field and drinking wine from vines I walked past that morning: perfection. But why does it taste so good? There are two explanations: one official and mainly false; the other, possibly helpful. The 'official' answer, found in all good books on food and wine, is that my sense of taste has matched the microclimate of the local area to the required growing conditions experienced by the produce I am now tasting. And this explanation seems plausible, for I, and pedants like me, know all too well that our insistence on taking back to our homes that same cheese and identical bottle of wine is doomed: it just doesn't taste the same away from the place that created it. So, something is going on, but I doubt it's just the change in the wind direction or saline quality of the air, or even the personal relaxation I bring on holiday but accidentally leave at the airport on my way home. No, I think what's missing when I get the cheese and wine back is my immediate connection with the creative people from the fields behind the restaurant or the vineyard I could see up the hill. What would you reply if asked by the owner of that little restaurant: "Do you want the local wine or the equally good stuff from the next commune?" "Local, of course." Of course, but why? For you know that if you were sitting in the next commune's restaurant facing the same question, you'd choose that local and if a hundred miles away, that local. We love to touch creativity.

Years ago we filled autograph books. Now, we look to selfies with our creative heroes as proof that we are close to creativity, with as little as possible separating it from us. If that means it's a bit ragged round the edges, a bit imperfect, then fine. In fact it's better, for it proves it's the product of human creativity, not a machine that churns out repetitive perfection twenty-four hours a day without a smidgen of emotion.

The Ikea sideboard. In recent years, the company has tried placing little posters next to its more expensive pieces of furniture showing potential customers the designer's photograph and telling us a bit about him or her and the origins of the product. Sensible. Ikea clearly recognised the unhelpful distance they had separating designer from shopper: the inevitable bureaucracy of planning and approving a new product; the manufacturing process; the quality assurance mechanisms; the marketing procedures; and the logistics of actually getting that sideboard into the shop. Ikea was wise to have realised that all this diminishes the emotional value to the customer of that piece of furniture and therefore lowers the price that can be charged for it. The photograph, designer's name and biog. proudly displayed in the shop is surely an attempt to leap over all those impediments to the communication of creativity: an attempt, metaphorically, to print the creative's hand on the shop wall in the hope that another human being will accept that offer of intimacy and place his or her own right hand on top; whilst the left reaches for a credit card.

In this Ikea paragraph I've suggested that an item's value to the purchaser is related to the degree of intimacy he or she feels with the creator of the piece, and that this is reflected in the price that the seller can demand for it. The fine art market takes this principle extremely seriously, judging that a faked painting, pretending to be the work of a great artist, is virtually worthless. I used to be puzzled at this decision, for that same painting may well have fooled experts for generations and have hung proudly on the walls of a major gallery. So yes, okay, it's now been discovered to be a fake, but that hasn't altered by a single brushstroke the way it looks, so surely it's still a great picture; the experts repeatedly said so before just re-assigning its authorship. All true; indeed the painting hasn't changed, but our relationship with it – and through it – certainly has changed, irrevocably. We had thought, whilst gazing at it on the gallery wall for all those credulous years, that we were peering through the canvas to an ever-deepening relationship with the human being who created it. On discovering that it's a fake, that trusting relationship is broken and we realise we've been speaking not to the creator, but simply to a mimic able to ape the voice, not the creativity, of the artist whose name is fraudulently asserted at the bottom of the canvas. Our supposed intimacy with the creative human being has been shown to be an illusion; and it's for that intimacy that the collector of creative objects is eager to pay. Betrayed, the object is indeed worthless. So, what has all this to do with your creative colleagues at work?

It is hardly surprising that my overall conclusion is that companies selling the creativity of its employees should be aware of this possible 'intimacy gap' between creative and customer, and should, like Ikea, attempt to limit or mitigate its effects. Of course, the methods used will vary from organisation to organisation and probably product to product, but one may frequently be seen. Action based on an understanding that creativity unencumbered by the traditional bureaucracy of organisational life can shout louder and deeper, more clearly and more convincingly than can creativity strangled by procedures designed not for creativity but organisational convenience and compliance with what worked okay last time. Not only will unnecessary bureaucracy and tradition depress the quality and quantity of creativity produced – as argued in Chapter 8 *Why do I do what I do?* – but it will inevitably attenuate and even gag the profitable, delightful and intimate conversation a creative should have with his or her ultimate patron: the customer. If the purchasers feel they are simply recipients of anonymous and mechanistic manufacturing, rather than active participants in a creative relationship, they are likely to look elsewhere for their next purchase; for the company has offered no handprint for the customer to match.

CONCLUSIONS

This chapter draws on the summaries of previous chapters, as checklists. The first list is for line-managers of creative colleagues; the second and third are directed more at an employing organisation's senior leaders. These checklists are offered in the hope that you find them a useful diagnostic toolkit to identify strengths and weaknesses in working with creative colleagues.

Line-managers of creatives are Facilitators with many hats, outlined below. They are…

Talent scouts who match the right colleagues to the right projects, so that creatives are stretched and excited by intrinsic motivation.

Brief maestros who formulate clear, but open, project briefs.

Resource gurus: allocators of people, time and money etc.

Space-makers who make room for their colleagues' creativity but don't attempt to control that creativity. It'll look a bit chaotic.

Creativity connoisseurs whose excitement comes from the quality of creativity their colleagues produce. They value their creatives in proportion to the quality of their creativity.

Protectors who don't let criticism of new-born creative ideas appear too early. They protect creatives from extrinsic organisational motivations and create space for the saturation-incubation-illumination process to unfold naturally.

Intermediaries who translate their creative colleagues' work to senior management, and organisational objectives to the creatives.

Diplomats aware of the need for sensitivity, but also honesty, in their intermediary role.

Seers who predict that highly creative ideas generally come from individuals, not teams. They accept the impossibility of planning in any detail the process of saturation, incubation and illumination.

Risk-takers comfortable in a culture of experimentation – including failure – indeterminate outcomes and divergence from the status quo.

Patrons: fans of their colleagues' creativity, but also eager to challenge their zones of comfort.

Judges who measure their creative colleagues' performance only by the quality of the creativity they produce, not by its process of creation, its reception within the company, customers' views or by eventual commercial success or failure. This requires managerial courage and trust, and, from the creative colleagues, the acceptance of responsibility for their own work.

Statesmen and stateswomen who resist using the volume of applause as a guide to the value of a creative piece of work, and who are aware that their craft is changing.

Savants skilled at judging potential creativity through the dazzle of a charismatic colleague.

Wow! We're asking a lot from our managers! How might the long list be summarised? Hard-line creative experts who consider creativity to be a rare and innate gift might propose that effective managers allow creatives to do the work they were born to do. But I, someone who considers creativity to be a universal attribute of human intelligence, prefer: *effective managers facilitate creativity wherever it appears and link it to organisational aspirations.*

Two checklists for senior leaders:

Values

For high level creativity to flourish, an employing organisation must have…

*   Attractive and sincerely held corporate values and purpose. These will often be rooted in a passion for what it does rather than simply in making money.

*   Senior managers who care about, and are interested in, what it creates and the colleagues who create it.

*   Senior managers with sufficient resources, time and creative

judgement to allow them to recognise, and insist upon, high levels of creativity.

- Financial resources to invest in recruiting and nurturing the creativity of diverse and divergent colleagues bringing myriad languages, customs, ideas and world views.

- Senior managers tolerant of non-conformity.

- An appetite for constant company transition, creating an awareness that everything is provisional: a creativity aphrodisiac.

- Leaders who cherish creativity as a resource different from other inputs, requiring informed and sensitive managing.

Operations

For creativity to flourish, the employing organisation must have operational processes that…

- Manage the inevitable tension between creative freedom and operational control.

- Allow the often unpredictable characteristics of creativity to determine how creativity is to be managed and do not permit incompatible management methods to define the creative process itself. The resulting management structures and styles will thus support creativity rather than attack it. Life might sometimes appear anarchic.

- Recognise the spectrum linking problem-solving to significant creativity and understand how to use the different management interventions required at different points on that creativity spectrum.

- Respect the importance to highly creative colleagues of intrinsic motivation; and creativity's vulnerability to extrinsic motivations.

- Recognise the dangers of bureaucratically generated gaps separating the creative idea from the customer's perception. A significant value to the purchaser resides in his or her perceived proximity to the creative spark.

And a summary of these summary lists, and indeed of this entire book?

TURN ME

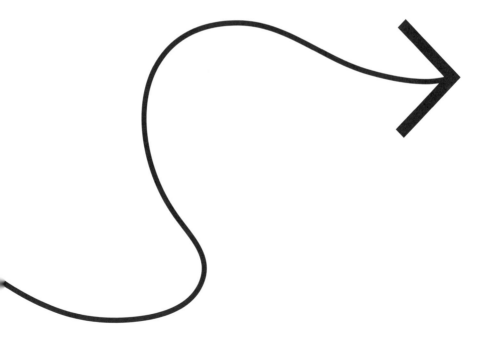

LET THE CREATIVES JUST GET ON WITH IT!

(...AS FAR AS YOU CAN.)

GOODNIGHT

[Myths can stick to creatives, especially after their deaths. In 1802, an obscure composer, Johann Nikolaus Forkel, added to the chatter already surrounding J. S. Bach's life and works through the publication of the master's first biography.[1]]

Dear Father

I hope this letter will be short. If it ends after just a few sentences you should congratulate rather than criticise me, I'll have successfully got the Count to sleep! But I have several candles – don't worry they're the cheap ones – just in case I'm in for a long night.

I miss my little bed back in Danzig, too small for me now of course, but that lovely smell from your workshop, the smell of music coming up through the floorboards, a sleepy smell, my old bed. Is it still there or have you made it into a harpsichord yet? My bed, my own childhood bed; always warm. I buried myself in the fleece so that I couldn't hear Mother crying.

"Goldberg! One of my variations if you please!" Well, I did warn you, Father.

[1]

Whether Forkel's account is reliable seems doubtful, yet provocatively so, for his 'truths' provide a model for a little further myth-making, and perhaps a summary of how best to work with creative colleagues.

Not too bad. I played the seventh variation, the little gigue. Really easy and quite calming. He got back to sleep quickly, dreaming of his latest conquest I imagine. She's called Augusta I think, but it doesn't matter if I'm wrong, there'll be a different one next week. Yes, he was starting to drop off as I was getting near the end, so I repeated the second half on the lute stop so I could hear his movement, you know, that staccato twitching of limbs just before sleep. His bed creaks a bit in sympathy and I can hear it if I'm playing quietly. But I wasn't certain he was asleep so I kept on playing, not with the Master's next variation; I would have to have stopped to get the right page and that would certainly have woken the Count. No, I improvised a bit, still using Master Bach's bass line of course, but to my own ideas. Then, I confess, I just kept playing to my own command and didn't bother listening for the Count's twitches. Just caught up in my music, I'd forgotten it was my job.

The first day of March tomorrow, 'heralding my illustrious birthday'. Do you remember my saying that every March 1st? You laughed and said I had 'ideas above my rank'. Well, you were wrong dear Father, because here I am, none other than harpsichordist to the Russian Ambassador to Saxony! Does Mother still make those little nutty biscuits on my birthday – their smell always reminded me of the varnish you use – like eating music. If she still manages to make them, could you send me some? Fifteen of course; the ones in the shape of little hearts. Then she'd sprinkle…

"Goldberg!"

I spoke too soon, he woke up! So I started playing him a new piece by one of Master Bach's sons, Wilhelm. I've been having some composition lessons from him. (So many children, and the Count too, lots of them, though most of these don't bear his name or are set to inherit his money! So many healthy children.) Anyway, I got a bit into the new piece and the Count stopped me, "No Goldberg, play one of my variations." And, as he said 'my', he swung his left leg out of the bed and stamped it on the floor. I knew then I'd be in for a long stint, so I played number 24 – the canon at the octave, the slow one; it takes a long time.

You know, for all his faults as a man – and he's certainly got a few of those! – he can tell if a piece of music is any good or not. One afternoon he and his latest amour were dining, and he asked me to play for them as they ate. I chose a prelude by the Master. He loved it, she just said, "Not really very tuneful", so I continued with some drivel arranged from a silly little Vivaldi concerto. "So much better, really pretty!" The Count said nothing, but that was the last we saw of her! I can't blame her too much though, she was just following the tastes of today. Not many of us still appreciate Master Bach's music, it takes too much work for most people. I wonder why fashions…

"Goldberg!"

I'm definitely in for a long night, he was wide awake. It took four variations to get him over! Yes, four out of the thirty. Now, who in their right mind writes thirty variations on a little sarabande? No one, certainly not Master Bach's sons. They might knock out a few but then they'd give up. Master Bach doesn't give up but insists on examining that childish little dance over and over again, finding there a fugue, loads of canons, a gigue, an overture, and a quodlibet; the lot. What kind of a composer has the determination to do that thirty times when a set of eight would be impressive enough? He's obsessed; well, not normal anyway.

Do you know what he's working on now? He told me when I was in Leipzig a few weeks ago that he's just finishing a second complete set of preludes and fugues in every major and minor key! So that'll be 48 in all. Well, I'm planning to write a dance in every key – it's my kind of nod to him, I owe him so much, but that's where I'll stop – twenty-four is definitely enough. How lost in music do you have to be to have so much to say in it?

I'm not talking about planning performances, worrying about whether anyone will like it, or even whether it will command a good fee. No, none of those. I think the Master gets lost in the notes themselves, how they work, how they live together, how they disagree, fall in love and create new notes. Surprising he has the time to produce so many real children! Sorry Father, I know you don't approve of such coarseness, but I've noticed that the more aristocratic the house the more bass the morals. Before coming here I'd have guessed the opposite. There was one evening when I was walking past the Count's chamber when I…

"Goldberg!"

These cheap candles are nearly finished. I'll have to end this letter soon. I wonder how long until dawn. Well, it wasn't the dawn that woke him this time, a troubled conscience maybe, but no signs of day through his windows. I played the 'overture', variation sixteen, this time, the one in that old French manner that master Bach still loves and everybody else has forgotten.

You know, I do wonder sometimes what the Master would compose if he weren't stuck in his church organ loft in Leipzig. He hardly ever gets to meet new people with new ideas and doesn't travel much. I know he's sent lots of new music – he even uses it in his pieces sometimes – but I don't think he can often meet new people to just chat about music, new ideas, new anything really. He's really out of touch with what's going on. His sons are much more up to date in the stuff they write. I know the Master loves them, he often talks about them, but I bet he doesn't think much of the new style they use. After all his lessons too! There's so little real counterpoint in it, just a nod sometimes with a few bars of imitation to get the piece started, but it fades away so soon. Ask Wilhelm to write a proper fugue? Don't waste your breath! A French Overture? I doubt he can remember what one is!

Yes, the Master's trapped in his work, a new cantata every week for his church. It must be horrific to go to bed on Sunday night knowing that the next day you've got to start producing next

Sunday's. But that's his job, he agreed to it and they're the rules he must follow. I go along to St Thomas' as often as I can, and his cantatas are always more than good enough, but their quality does vary. It's odd, but when there's one that's not so good, I always think the organ pieces he improvises during the service seem especially good. It's as if he's making up for the music he was ordered to write with something he just wants to produce. Well, that variation I just played the Count was something the Master really wanted to compose. What a fantastic piece, and the whole set – all thirty of them – is like that, full of 'compositional rules' but sort of self-imposed, not dictated by his employer. And perhaps Father, perhaps that's why the Count's variations came to be composed. Maybe the Master saw them as an escape?

Well, that's just me dreaming perhaps, but what actually happened was that the Count took me to see Master Bach whilst we were visiting Leipzig. I already knew him of course; he'd given me a few lessons after hearing me play. Gosh, that seems so long ago now but it's only three or four years. You remember, it must have been you or Mother who took me to his lodgings. But it was probably you. You usually took me to all those grand houses with everyone telling you what a miracle son you had. Did that make you glad or sad? I hope glad, and I'm really pleased it brought you some money. But now, looking back on it, it sometimes makes me a bit sad, for perhaps, just perhaps, I was at the height of my career back then. To have reached my summit aged ten leaves a very long time to slide down the other side, that is unless I'm taken early of course. And there's illness here, a maidservant has just left with a dreadful cough. I do worry.

Anyway, the variations – the Count and I visited Master Bach, and the Count asked him to compose some keyboard pieces for me to play. And that was it, really, that's all he said. Nothing about how long they must be, didn't say how hard they should be to play – although, as they were for me, the Master knew they could be as taxing as he wished – and he didn't state a date they were to be finished. That was all, just that he wanted to be cheered up by the pieces in his sleepless nights. No details, not even that they should be in the form of a theme and variations. And there was one other thing that really surprised me. There was no agreement of the price to be paid. I suppose the Master, knowing the Count's wealth and generosity, wasn't worried by this. But it is interesting that the subject was never mentioned. The Master was certainly not taking the commission just to obtain the fee. Did you ever think about the money when you were showing me off as a child to the rich people of Danzig?

So the commission was offered by the Count and accepted by Master Bach, if 'commission' is quite the right word for such a casual arrangement. But the Master was right not to worry about the fee. When the Master delivered the finished manuscript to us and had got me to play it through to him and the Count (don't forget my old nickname The Note Eater, it certainly came in handy with that bit of sight-reading!) after I'd finished playing, the Count nodded to a servant who lifted a heavy object covered in a gold embroidered cloth from a side table and carried it to the Count who removed the cloth with a flourish and presented Master Bach with "A golden berg for Goldberg's composer." It was a gold goblet filled with a mountain of gold Louis d'or, at least a hundred. A gold-berg indeed.

So it has always rather surprised me that the Count calls the variations 'his'. Shouldn't they be mine? I know what you're thinking Father, whoever pays for them owns them; so they're the Count's. But I don't think that's quite right. First they're Bach's, second mine and only third the Count's; he should be satisfied with having brought their creation about. Isn't that honour enough?

Anyway, all those rules that the Count failed to give the Master, must, I think, have been a big relief from the clear duties of his normal weekly work composing for the choirs in Leipzig. 'Got to use the right text for next Sunday'; 'got to be performable after only a few rehearsals'; 'mustn't be too long (the congregation has complained recently)'; 'mustn't be too short (St Thomas' is the main church in Leipzig after all)…'

So many orders to obey! So many rules that are really nothing to do with the actual music, but which stop you writing what you secretly know you could write. It's just like… well Father, you know I'm still composing some pieces myself, trio sonatas and a cantata actually. Don't worry, I'm not neglecting my playing. I know that's what pays my salary. Well, I'm sorry to say this but they're not really very good, even by the modest standards of Wilhelm Bach. And I think it's the Master's fault. I'm trying to follow his way of composing – his counterpoint, his harmony, his ways of changing key; they're sort of rules and goals I'm trying to follow, and it's just not working because I'm not him and never will be him. By now I should have got all that stuff sort of absorbed, built into me so I'm no longer aware of it. Then perhaps I could be myself for a change, free to write the music I hear in my head rather than sounds fit for another's nature.

Yes, I do worry Father. A good harpsichordist at ten years old is a phenomenon, the same talent at fifteen is less interesting. What will I do when I'm twenty? I need my compositions to grow up and leave home.

You made Anna's little coffin didn't you. I remember you picking out the pieces of the best wood from your store, joining them together with such care even though they would be seen only by worms. Then you carried it – only a touch heavier – to the church, Mother and I walked behind you. it was getting dark and…

"Goldberg!"

Just the sarabande this time, that's all he wanted. Just the little aria that starts and ends the work. Very simple really. The Count sometimes plays it himself. Easy to play, yes, but full of possibilities, pregnant. As I'm playing it I imagine it's about to give birth to all its sons and daughters. So it's not actually 'easy' at all, for it contains so much knowledge of what is to come. Anyway, I took the first page of music and started playing, but he stopped me. "No Goldberg, play the last time it appears, not the first." "But it's the same thing!" I knew I shouldn't have spoken in this way, but the Count is good about that sort of thing. When we're in Music's world outside rules don't apply. So I turned to the last page of the copy I've made and started the sarabande once again. "That's better," he mumbled as he – finally! – went back to sleep. And I agree with him, it is different at the end, and perhaps that's what the Count was looking for. After all those variations, coming home to what you recognise, older and knowing a little more. A slow, stately sarabande at the end of a sleepless night, a long life; or even a short one. Anna would have liked it. Perhaps when I'm next home. Tell Mother I love her.

Your affectionate son
Johann

PS my last candle is about to go out, but I think I can just see, if I peer ... yes, I think, just ... yes, on the horizon over there, maybe, yes, some light. The Count will sleep now, and so will I.

Goodnight Father.

ACKNOWLEDGEMENTS

I've already, in the introduction, gratefully noted the work of Gordon Torr. To complete the top trio I add Teresa Amabile and Ken Robinson. Their seminal works are listed in *Sources cited*. Although these experts are key to my thinking, I'm certain they won't mind sharing the applause with the many creative colleagues with whom I've worked for more than forty years. Through experiencing their creativity, being amazed at their creative processes, by watching, listening, celebrating their successes, and sensing their fears, I have picked up what little I know about creativity, and how to be their plausibly effective colleague and manager.

My gratitude also goes to Isabelle Desjeux for permission to reproduce her art work in Chapter 14 *The creative process*, and to the publishers of *Training Journal*, in whose pages early versions of the chapters now entitled *Solo, Artiste, Molotov, Playful* and *Courageous companies: creative chaos* first appeared. Heartfelt thanks go to Amanda Bergius, my editor, and finally, to Marcus Myles, the designer and illustrator of this book and creator of my website and brand.

But most of all, admiration and gratitude to my wife, Maureen, and daughter, Flora, who have taught me that creativity is needed at home too!

SOURCES CITED

Amabile, T. M. and Conti, R. (1997). Environmental determinants of work motivation, creativity, and innovation: The case of R&D downsizing. *Technical Innovation: Oversights & Foresights* 111-126.
DOI: https://doi.org/10.1017/CBO9780511896613.009
Cambridge University Press.

Amabile, T. M. and Khaire, M. (2008). Creativity and the Role of the Leader. *Harvard Business Review* [online] 86 (10); 100-109, 142. https://hbr.org/2008/10/creativity-and-the-role-of-the-leader

Amabile, T. M. (1996). *Creativity in Context.* Colorado: Westview Press.

Anwar, M. N., Shamim-ur-Rasool, S. and Haq, R. (2012). A Comparison of Creative Thinking Abilities of High and Low Achievers Secondary School Students. *International Interdisciplinary Journal of Education* 1(1); 1-6.

Benjamin, W. (1935). *Das Kunstwerk im Zeitalter seiner technischen Reproduzierbarkeit.* Translated by Underwood, J. A. (2008). *The Work of Art in the Age of Mechanical Reproduction.* London: Penguin.

Chamorro-Premuzic, T. (2017). *Working With Creatives: A Short Guide for Everyone Else.* Fast Company [online] 30 October 2017. Available at: https://www.fastcompany.com/40484057/creative-people-are-hard-to-work-with-heres-what-to-do-about-it/

Chamorro-Premuzic, T. (2013). Seven Rules for Managing Creative-But-Difficult People. *Harvard Business Review* [online] 02 April, 2013. Available at https://hbr.org/2013/04/seven-rules-for-managing-creat/

Davis, H. and Scase, R. (2000). *Managing Creativity: the dynamics of work and organization.* Buckingham, Open University Press.

Dolan, L. (2020). *Working with creatives.* Business-success-blog. https://keap. com/business-success-blog/business-management/leadership/how-to-do-great-work-with-these-4-creative-types/

Elsbach, K. D., Brown-Saracino, B. and Flynn, F. J. (2015). Collaborating with Creative Peers. *Harvard Business Review* [online] October. https://hbr. org/2015/10/collaborating-with-creative-peers.

Forkel, N. J. (1802). *Über Johann Sebastian Bachs Leben, Kunst und Kunstwerke.* Für patriotische Verehrer echter musikalischer Kunst. Leipzig.

Gino, F. (2014). *Dishonesty and Creativity: Two Sides of the Same Coin?* https:// www.psychologicalscience.org/news/releases/dishonesty-and-creativity-two-sides-of-the-same-coin.html/

Hackley, C. and Kover, A. J. (2007). The trouble with creatives: Negotiating creative identity in advertising agencies. *International Journal of Advertising* [online] 6(1); 63-78. https://www.researchgate.net/publication/232478540_ The_trouble_with_creatives_Negotiating_creative_identity_in_advertising_ agencies

Hathaway, S. R. & McKinley, J. C. (revised 1951). *Minnesota Multiphasic Personality Inventory; manual.* New York: Psychological Corporation.

Kampylis, P. (2010). Redefining Creativity – Analyzing Definitions, Collocations, and Consequences. *The Journal of Creative Behavior* 44(3); 191-214. https://www.academia.edu/18317882/Redefining_Creativity_Analyzing_ Definitions_Collocations_and_Consequences?auto=citations&from=cover_ page

Martinsen, Ø. L. (2011). The Creative Personality: A Synthesis and Development of the Creative Person Profile. *Creativity Research Journal* [online] 23(1); 185-202. https://www.tandfonline.com/doi/abs/10.1080/10400419.20 11.595656

Mesiti, P. (2017). *Why Creative People Struggle to Work in Conventional Jobs.* [online] Mesiti.com 03 December. https://mesiti.com/why-creative-people-struggle-to-work-in-conventional-jobs/#:~:text=They%20have%20a%20tendency%20to,make%20for%20poor%20team%20members.

Moga, B. (2017). *How to Manage and Lead Creative Teams.* ActiveCollab blog. https://activecollab.com/blog/collaboration/how-to-manage-and-lead-creative-teams/

Robinson, K. (2011). *Out of our minds: Learning to be Creative.* Oxford: Capstone Publishing Limited.

Siegler, B. (2018). *DEAR CLIENT, THIS BOOK WILL TEACH YOU HOW TO GET WHAT YOU WANT FROM CREATIVE PEOPLE. SINCERELY, BONNIE SIEGLER.* New York: Artisan.

Torr, G. (2008). *MANAGING CREATIVE PEOPLE: Lessons in Leadership for the Ideas Economy.* Chichester: Wiley.

Vincent, L. C. and Kouchaki, M. (2015). Why Creative People Are More Likely to Be Dishonest. *Harvard Business Review* [online] 23 November. https://hbr.org/2015/11/why-creative-people-are-more-likely-to-be-dishonest/

Ward, J., Thompson-Lake, D., Ely, R. and Kaminski, F. (2008). Synaesthesia, creativity and art: what is the link? *British Journal of Psychology* 99;127-41.

Weber, M. (1926). *Politik als Beruf* Edited by Reitter, P. and Wellmon, C; translated by Searls, D. (2020) *Charisma and Disenchantment: the Vocation Lectures.* New York: New York Review of Books.

.

Professor Alastair Pearce is an authority
on creativity. He has led university-level
institutions in both Europe and South East
Asia dedicated to producing innovative and
skilful graduates now working around the
world in fields from performing arts and
fashion to marketing and industrial design.

Alastair Pearce is a charismatic speaker,
in demand from major companies
whose work depends on the creativity of
employees. Through his presentations and
workshops, organisations – of any size
and commercial sector – understand how
their creativity can be nurtured, and, just
as importantly, how traditional models of
management often undermine creativity.

In 2020 Prof. Pearce formed the
consultancy Working With Creatives. He
remains its director.

Workingwithcreatives.co.uk